Future Ivy

Ω

Your guide to college applications, personal essays, and standing out in Ivy League college admissions

by

Amy Jin

Copyright © 2021 Amy Jin

Ω

All rights reserved. No part of this book may be reproduced or used in any manner without the prior written permission of the copyright owner, except for the use of brief quotations in a book review.

To request permissions, contact the publisher at Ivyleagueguidellc@gmail.com

ISBN: 9798746520777

First paperback edition January 2020.
Published by Smart Jumpstart Llc

Disclaimer

The events and conversations in this book have been set down to the best of the author's ability, although some names and details have been changed to protect the privacy of individuals.

Neither Amy Jin (AJ), nor its partners, principals, consultants, represent that the student will gain admission to any particular college or university and neither AJ, nor its partners, principals, consultants is responsible in any way for the student's failure to gain such admission. Due to the ever increasing number of applicants and the declining number of admits, no student can be assured of admission at any particular college or university, no matter how strong that student is academically. Institutions may change policies or courses of which we may not be aware and in such cases no liability shall accrue on us for such changes of which we are not made aware at the time of offering advice or when such changes are made after a student gains admission. Students and parents should carry out due diligence before making a commitment.

Praise

"For high schooler's looking for an empathetic ear, immigrant success story, and a systematic approach to college admissions, look no further than Ms. Jin's book geared towards empowering students to reach for the stars."
— Dr. Michele Hernandez, former Dartmouth Assistant Director of Admissions, founder of Top Tier Admissions

"This is a must-read for any high schooler overwhelmed by the college process."
— Tom Kuegler, Huffington Post writer and founder of The-Post Grad Survival Guide

"A game changing admissions book - Fun, eye opening and deeply informative."
— Madeline Mann, former USC admissions, founder of Self Made Millennial (top 5 career YouTube channel)

"You'll read Future Ivy. Then you'll hope that your competition isn't reading this. It's that good."
— Rachel Richards, bestselling author of Money Honey and former financial advisor

"As a high school student, Amy undoubtedly made her applications POP! The good news for you: she's condensed it into a practical, seven step guide for success."
— Brett Sklove, high school counselor with 25 years of experience

"Amy has done something remarkable here, turning the art of standing out in admissions into a clear, 7 step process."
— Chris Price, dad of 3 Ivy League grads, financial advisor
"It was easy- I followed Amy's system and got in!"

— Jessica, admitted to Harvard early action

"Actionable, easy to follow blueprint for making your Ivy League dreams come true."
— Anna Sabino, bestselling author of *Your Creative Career*, branding coach

"Action-oriented and inspiring, Future Ivy is a trusted friend on any college hopeful's path to greatness."
— Morgan Hendrix, Wild + Brave, high performance coach

Amy Jin has written a must-read primer for anyone considering Ivy League schools…Read this book - and learn from one of the best."
— Wendy Scharfman, executive communication coach

"Amy's knowledge, insight, and competence are all apparent in this book. Her 7 step process will give you the skills (and confidence!) to achieve admissions into any school of your choice."
-Erin Richter-Weikum, Research Librarian at American Public University System

"This book blew my mind. It's a riveting read, full of instantly actionable advice."
— MicKallyn Elis, parent and financial coach of The Cash Coach

"Amy is an incredibly precise and empathetic communicator, and is able to break down a complex, opaque, and harrowing process into concrete steps you can take to maximize your chances of success. These lessons also become skills you can apply elsewhere in your life, at school, at work, and beyond."
—Jon Rahoi, senior staff software engineer at Credit Karma, public speaking and computer science teacher

"You don't realize how far away college is and how much preparation you need. Amy helps you get a head start on everyone else that doesn't know anything."
—Olivia, high school student

"Amy's book completely changes the college application landscape, making the Ivy League possible for students who don't come from a typical, wealthy Ivy League background."
—Jessica Zhang, Cornell University student

Dedication

♥

To My Future Ivy students

Continue To Dream, Aim, And Soar!

Table of Contents

Introduction 1
    Why + how you should read this book 1

Chapter 1 10
    Who is an Ivy League school right for? 10

Chapter 2 18
    Why go to an Ivy? 18

Chapter 3 25
    Be different 25

Chapter 4 31
    How to stay motivated 31

Chapter 5 38
    How to stand out to the Ivy League with the ACHIEVE system 38

Chapter 6 46
    Step 1 of Achieve – Aim for As in advanced classes 46
    Skill: The 4-year advanced schedule 53

Chapter 7 63
    Step 2 of Achieve - Conduct an Activity Audit 63
    Skill: The Time Audit 66

Chapter 8 73
    Step 3 of Achieve - Help your teacher help you 73
    Skill: The Avocado Toast Method 76

Chapter 9 83
    Step 4 of ACHIEVE - Ignite your interests 83
    Skill: Online Outreach 87

Chapter 10 99
    Step 5 of ACHIEVE 99
    Skill: Finding your theme 110

Chapter 11 116
    Step 6 of ACHIEVE - Validate your credibility 116
    Skill: resume writing for impact 120

Chapter 12 .... *127*
    Step 7 of ACHIEVE – Earn your target SAT/ACT score 127
    Skill: the accountability buddy 132

Chapter 13 .... *142*
    Putting it all together 142

Chapter 14 .... *151*
    Building a team 151

Chapter 15 .... *158*
    What we know about Ivy League admissions 158

Chapter 16 .... *167*
    College essays 167
    Why you should care about essays 169
    Types of essays 171
    The Writing Process 172
    How to Brainstorm Your Essay Topic 175
    How to structure your essay 177
    Supplemental Essays 179

Chapter 17 .... *183*
    The Finishing Touches 183

Chapter 18 .... *192*
    The final stretch 192

Chapter 19 .... *199*
    NEXT STEPS 199
    Closing Remarks 202
    Appendix A 204
    ACHIEVE system checklist 204

INTRODUCTION

Σ

Why + how you should read this book

Let's pretend you've just been accepted into the school of your dreams. You've thought about this day for months, maybe even years, so it doesn't seem real yet. You look at the poster on your bedroom wall and can't believe that you'll soon be walking amongst the statues and buildings named after founding fathers and Nobel prize winners. You know your parents will be ecstatic for you and most likely will cry when they send you off to your freshman year. You might cry too, but for different reasons. It probably hasn't sunk in yet how big of a deal this is.

Maybe you're still thinking about all the challenges you had to overcome, all the late nights studying, stressing about essays, and extracurricular work. Maybe you've suddenly started second guessing yourself on whether you can make it and survive by yourself or compete with the top students in the world.

Let me reassure you that you've just finished what is probably the most stressful part of the entire college process. Ivy League schools (such as Harvard, Columbia, or Penn) and other top-tier institutions have below 10% acceptance rates. That is beyond bananas. There are lotteries out there with better odds. But after that, you've made it! The icing on the cake is that you are far more likely to graduate from said top university than be accepted in the first place. Seriously, for me and most of my classmates, Harvard's course-load was way easier and much more fun than public high school. So, if you're in, you're done with the hardest part!

Back in the real world, I want to let you know that this doesn't have to be a hypothetical. Your decision to pick up this book tells me you are an ambitious student who wants to go to an Ivy League university, or maybe you are a parent thinking of this book for your child. Well, you are in the right place. I've worked with many students who set their sights on a top college, established a plan of action, and followed through to make it happen. It seems easier said than done, but bear with me: this book will outline the steps you can follow to greatly increase your chances of getting an acceptance letter and gain a competitive edge over applicants with similar stats.

When I was in high school, the college application process totally consumed my life. I remember struggling immensely (as the oldest child in an immigrant family) with the most important questions and decisions of my life. I often wondered: "Where do I go for college?" Do I even have a chance at an Ivy? How do I stand out among applicants with the same stats/grades? How do I even start to apply? How can I beat the odds? And of course the underlying, unspoken question, "How in the world do I get accepted?" This book aims to answer all these questions and more.

You may be feeling overwhelmed by all of this. I remember my grandma and my parents would gossip about what all the other "smart" kids in the neighborhood were accomplishing, like missionary trips, science awards, and all the top schools they got into. It wasn't very helpful, and it left me confused about how I was going to show that I was different and unique.

If you're worried about whether you can get into your dream college, I want to put those fears to rest. You can do this. You just need the right person to explain it to you. Someone who has been through the process and has a track record of getting into the Ivy League, who has coached students that got into Harvard, MIT, Caltech, Berkeley, and more. I want you to have all the opportunities that the Ivy League offers. Since graduating from an Ivy League school, I've had the amazing chance to meet Fortune 500 CEOs, intern on TV sets, and receive constant job offers.

So, that's what I'm here for. I know you have a dream to make your parents proud, or to create a better life for you and your family, or just to make an impact, and I want to guide you on that journey with this book.

My story

I'm Amy Jin (@ivyleagueguide), and I help students stand out to their dream colleges through social media. When I was applying to college, I was overwhelmed with stress. I had no clue about the application process in the U.S. and worried whether I was on the "right track" to stand out to my dream college.

I had known since childhood that I wanted to go to a top college, either for law or something medical on my parents' strong suggestions, but I had no clue how to go about it. I had no idea how to write the personal essay, take the SATs, or fill out the financial aid applications. Luckily, I am known to be resourceful, and through sheer determination, asking lots of questions, and hard work, I ended up pulling it all together and getting into my dream college, Harvard University.

In high school, I learned that I had a knack for teaching when I turned my experience with debate into a club and tutored other students. Having learned the Ivy League application process, I realized I could pass this knowledge on to others as well. I created the ACHIEVE system to share the approach that got me into Harvard, helped me land a six-figure job, and has gotten me promoted. My friends begged me to share my secrets, and now I'm offering them to you.

Because I've lived through applications to top colleges and helped other students stand out, I have lots of personal stories and examples to share throughout this book. I hope that will help you see that you have a chance at the Ivy League too!

Why another admissions book?

I wrote this book because I don't want you to go through the same stress I went through. My parents immigrated here from China and had no idea how to help me stand out to an Ivy League school, study for the SAT, or fill out the FAFSA (the financial aid form). I had hoped the democratization of information (via Google) would have solved a lot of the stress of applying by now, but that hasn't happened. If anything, it's only been getting more and more complicated.

I graduated from Harvard in 2017, and today I'm shocked by the lack of information and assistance for students even with the endless free resources available on the internet. I want to help you deal with this insane information overload and be your guide during this process. I do it because I love to teach and coach students through essays, passion portfolios, and getting internships.

While I respect some of the college advice you can find on Reddit and many other college blogs, it's hard to know what's good advice, what advice will work for you, and how to apply what you're told. In fact, there's so much information out there these days that it practically takes an advanced degree just to understand the process of getting your first degree. I don't think it should be that complicated. You deserve to know how the college admission game works and how you can win. This book is a checklist of proven strategies that will help you do just that and set you up for an amazing career.

I've structured this book similar to the building of a house.

First, we build the foundation of the house which is your mindset. Your positive mindset and clear "why" will be the steel rods that strengthen the cement foundation against earthquakes, or stumbling blocks in the application process.

Then we put up the walls, windows, and roof of the house. This is where we'll need to reach into our tool kit and use the right tool for the job. I'll share with you a series of skills that will help you figure out if you are on the right track and how to stay on-track to getting into a top school.

Next, we'll need some advice with the furniture, painting, and interior decorating. While you will have all the skills you need at this point, I seriously recommend you don't do it alone. In fact, I recommend you build a support team that will help encourage and motivate you.

Lastly, in order to sell the house, we must take some good pictures, put it in the market, and advertise it. I'm going to show you how to get into the mind of an admissions officer when looking at your application and understand how you can stand out from the crowd. You will learn how to talk confidently about your achievements and make sure your application, essays, interviews, and letters of recommendation "wow" admissions and make them remember you when your application is in front of the committee.

To get you the best advice, I interviewed many Ivy league students, including the students I've coached, so that you have plenty of examples. If you really want to get the most out of this book, I encourage you to read each chapter twice and place the book in a visible spot. This book can be your guide to what's important in the college journey. You can earmark the pages that you want to refer back to and I recommend a highlighter to emphasize key examples and concepts. At the end of each chapter, I provide a summary and action items regarding those concepts. If you are reading the ebook, you can screenshot pages that you'd like to save.

The more you complete the action items the more likely you will get into your dream college. So buckle up, get your highlighters, and prepare to discover the secrets of not just surviving but thriving when you are applying to college.

Summary

* It's not your fault that you are lost in the college application process. It's because of information overload. To get the most out of this book, reread the chapters and complete the action steps.

Actions Steps:

- ☐ Say out loud "I can do this" 3x
- ☐ Find a visible spot where you can put the book so it serves as a daily reminder
- ☐ Check off these boxes when complete

Part 1

α

Foundation

Future Ivy

CHAPTER 1

α

Who is an Ivy League school right for?

When you think about the Ivy League, what do you think about? Is it Gilmore Girls and ivory towers? Full of rich, preppy, smart students? That's how I felt, because I didn't know many people who went to top schools.

When I was 10, I attended a Chinese bible study group where I got to speak to a real Harvard student, my neighbor's daughter, Lili. "I feel so dumb there," she grumbled as we walked upstairs where the other kids were. "Everyone is so much smarter than me at Harvard."

I was only in elementary school and thought that if she felt dumb there, I surely would also. You might feel the same way. Or maybe you wonder even if you get into the Ivy League of your dreams, whether you would do well? Would you be able to keep up?

I worried like this because although I came from a public school that had a decent AP (advanced) program, it just didn't compare to the top prep schools with the finest tutors. I thought I was going to be completely outclassed.

Will you feel dumb there?

Yes and no. You need to remember that you are going to school with the best and brightest students from all around the world. You may have been the top of your class, but now so will have all the other students there with you. If you focus only on one skill, like your abilities in physics, then you might feel dumb.

However, if you zoom out and realize that we are a combination of strengths and weaknesses and that no one is the same, then no, you won't feel dumb. For example, one of my classmates had perfect pitch and was a musical genius but struggled with serious procrastination, with teachers having to remind him 3+ times to turn in assignments. Another one of my classmates had the most eloquent and clear writing I'd ever seen, but had trouble with basic math.

We are all different.

Focus on your strengths and make friends with people who can complement your weaknesses. My strength is networking and connecting people, so I used this strength to match people who I thought would make great friends. I remember I had two friends who had similar interests in classical music, physics, and the German language. By the end of the meeting, they were finishing each other's sentences!

"It's hard to get in, but not hard to graduate," one of my Harvard classmates said to me during freshman year. At the time I was still in shock coming from high school and star-struck to be at Harvard, but eventually I found this quote to be true. For every class, you have office hours with the teachers' assistants on a weekly basis, you have access to peer tutors, and there were free tutoring centers for math and writing almost every day. Schools like Harvard are invested in your success once you are admitted.

I struggled with the open-ended homework that my Calculus B/C class gave me. I had taken the course in high school but it was way easier then. In high school, the teacher would lecture and give examples that were similar. In college, they teach you the basic principles but the homework would be four advanced questions. Now, instead of getting 30 easy questions for homework, I had four tough, theoretical questions. I sought out the help of my classmates and went to the math question center almost every day. With perseverance, I was able to get through the class and make friends, too.

If your strength is courage and gratitude, you could use your courage to go to your professor's office hours and your gratitude to send them a thank you email after the meeting. Building the friendship will make it easier to ask for help later. The truth is, as long as you ask for help when you are struggling, you can do well at an Ivy League. Struggling with a topic is normal; we can all use some help in certain classes.

Is everyone at the Ivies preppy?

Just as you may think the Ivy League is only for geniuses, I thought that I would be surrounded by preppy kids. I wanted to make a good impression and fit in, so I sheepishly researched Ivy League style and made lists of all the brands of jeans and sweaters that I needed.

Since I didn't have the money to pay full price for Ralph Lauren or Citizen For Humanity jeans, I stopped by the Goodwill in a nicer neighborhood. I was able to find cashmere sweaters for 9 bucks and brand new designer jeans for 15. Man, how I miss those deals.

When I got to Harvard, I was well-prepared with my stash of preppy clothes. I remember walking into the freshman dining hall, which looks like something straight out of Harry Potter, and realizing that I was wrong. I was the most overdressed, preppy person there. Most students wore t-shirts and nondescript jeans. Some people were dressed in sweatpants and sweatshirts and looked like they had just climbed out of bed. Coming from a California public school, where a lot of girls wore makeup and the guys shaved, I was shocked to see faces without makeup and guys who had grown out their beards in weird, month-based manliness challenges.

I realized then that Ivy League students don't get voted "best dressed" or "most chic" in their senior yearbooks. I realized that the preppy style I'd imagined was all a misconception. Fortunately, all my misguided preparation made me the best-dressed Harvard student anyone had met.

Is everyone at the Ivies rich?

While it may seem like the Ivy League is only for rich kids, that's actually far from the truth. The institutions do a great deal of work trying to recruit low income students and offer some of the most generous financial aid available to middle class families of all US universities.

For example, the average parent contribution at Harvard is only $12,000, since 55% of students receive financial aid.[1] This is based on your family's income, so search Harvard's net price calculator to see what your estimated cost would be. Most colleges have a similar financial aid calculator on their websites.

While the sticker price for an Ivy League education is crazy high, the true cost can be reasonable. For example, if you received no aid going to Yale in 2021, you'd pay ~$81,000 per year.[2] While some families can afford that sticker price, it's more than most Americans make in a whole year! In order to help more families, elite schools like Yale offer generous financial aid awards. If your family income in 2021 was $100,000-

---

[1] https://college.harvard.edu/financial-aid/how-aid-works
[2] https://finaid.yale.edu/costs-affordability/costs

$150,000, then you'd pay around $15,000 a year. Only 19% of the sticker price![3] And it would go down from there.

Some schools in the Ivy League also give financial aid to international students. For example, Columbia University offered 299 international students an average financial award of $71,069, and Harvard offered 605 international students an average financial award of $66,805.[4] Not all universities can afford to be this generous, so check on your dream college's financial aid website to see how much you would be predicted to get.

Ultimately, the Ivy League is no longer just for the rich. Most top schools have great financial benefits for lower and middle class students, even if you are international.

The Ivy League is not for everyone

While the Ivy League can still be for you even if you aren't rich, preppy, or a genius, it would be a difficult place for you if you struggle with academics.

We all have our strong subjects and weak subjects, and the honors/AP/IB classes are intended to challenge you, but if taking these hard classes is too overwhelming, it may be a sign that the Ivy League wouldn't be a great fit for you. And that's okay. There are many other great colleges out there.

The Ivy League will stretch your problem solving skills to their limit in many classes, so you'll need to ask for help. However, this is not

---

[3] https://finaid.yale.edu/costs-affordability/affordability
[4] https://www.usnews.com/education/best-colleges/the-short-list-college/articles/universities-that-offer-international-students-the-most-financial-aid

Future Ivy

like high school, where the teacher has 30 students per class and has the time to reach out to you for missing assignments or chat with you if you are failing. Some of the intro classes have hundreds of students, so you'll need to take the initiative to ask for help when struggling. Luckily, there are plenty of office hours with teachers' assistants, and your peers can be great study buddies.

Lastly, the Ivy League is not known for their mental health services. Being away from your family and friends is hard enough, so do your best to build a healthy mental foundation before going to college and invest time with your most supportive friends once you're there.

Summary

* In this first chapter, you busted the myths and misconceptions about the Ivy League, like that it's only for the rich, the preppy, and the geniuses.
* You learned that the sticker price of the Ivy League schools can be misleading, since there's lots of scholarships and financial aid that scales based on your family's income.
* At the same time, the Ivy League is not for everyone, and if you struggle to ask for help, you'll have a very tough time without your parents or high school teachers around.

Action Steps

- ☐ Look up the financial aid websites of the college you are applying to
- ☐ Figure out how much your predicted cost will be based on your family's income
- ☐ Write down 2 of your strengths

Future Ivy

CHAPTER 2

α

Why go to an Ivy?

"I don't think Harvard made that big of a difference," I told my coworker as we were taking our lunch break in the park.

"Amy, you don't understand how hard it can be to break into the tech industry without a brand name college," he said.

He told me about how he went to community college to get his computer science degree, and when he graduated, he had his friends at big tech companies internally forward his resume to the hiring managers. Here's how it went.

After a week

He got all rejection letters and no first-round interviews. So, he decided to see if adding a brand name college would make a difference to his resume.

Within an hour, he got an email back from the recruiter for a first-round interview. He didn't pursue the job (because that would be lying on your resume, which you could get fired for), but the point was clear. Changing just your university name to a top school name can open doors for you.

What made the difference?

I was astounded by this story. Yes, he did finally end up at the same tech company as I did, but I could see how my route to the job was easier and shorter.

Right out of college, I went into strategy consulting, helping companies grow their businesses by understanding the market trends and where they stood relative to their competitors. Landing a coveted consulting position was relatively easy, since lots of top consulting firms recruit on campus at most Ivy Leagues. Then, after 2 years, when I decided to change to the tech industry, it was very easy to get first-round interviews and ultimately land a high-paying job in tech.

Marc Andreessen, a venture capitalist and entrepreneur, explains in his A16z podcast that in the past, employers used lots of IQ and personality tests to screen candidates, but it became socially undesirable. Employers still wanted a way to screen for IQ and attention to detail, so they looked to the college name as a stand-in. This means that where you go to college influences how employers think about your intelligence and employability.

Meanwhile, my coworker spent many years in contractor roles without coveted benefits like paid time off, paid holidays, or healthcare and with fixed end dates. He had to prove himself before getting to be a full-time employee at a tech company.

Life is easier with an Ivy League degree

This shows two things. First, it's possible to get into a well-paid tech job even if you didn't go to a top school, but the route may be longer and harder. Second, brand college names like the Ivy League will help you get past the first round of resume screening and help you land more opportunities.

I also interviewed a student who went to an Ivy League college and then went to Stanford to do his PhD program. He mentioned that the credibility helps you get into grad school, too.

In addition to getting a credibility boost from your college's name, the Ivy League has a valuable alumni network. An alumni network is the group of people who went to the school and can offer the students of the school unique opportunities.

For example, Harvard's alumni network helped me land internships at a big consumer goods company, an executive recruiting firm, and a popular TV show, all while I was in college. One of my Harvard classmates founded a company with another Harvard student. This happens either by reaching out to the network yourself or the alumni coming back to the office of career services and offering the opportunity. I've found that people like to help those who are similar to them, so if you went to the same school they did, they'll be more likely to help you.

The Ivy League has more resources

When talking to some of my friends at UC Berkeley, I was surprised to hear that students on a day-to-day basis had to deal with a lack of funding at their school and that due to the size of the school, there was a prevalent sink-or-swim mentality. In fact, in order to address their money issues, UC Berkeley relies on more and more out-of-state students who pay higher tuition.[5]

---

[5] https://www.washingtonpost.com/news/grade-point/wp/2016/02/10/berkeley-is-facing-big-budget-trouble-painful-measures-ahead-for-nations-top-public-college/

In my mind, funding should be the least of your worries as a student, and the school should be ensuring that all students can focus on their grades and getting involved in the college community.

At Harvard, I found the common refrain, "It's hard to get in, but not hard to graduate," to be absolutely true. As long as you ask for help. For example, every freshman is introduced to tons of people who can support and help you. Every dormitory has a resident advisor (R.A.) who lives near you and has frequent study breaks with free snacks. You also have a peer mentor, an empathetic upperclassman who checks in with you and can relate to your experience.

On the academic side, you have your professors and teaching assistants (T.A.s) who hold regular, helpful office hours. You have the math resource center, which is staffed every night with eager math tutors and peers who can help you with homework, and you have the writing center, where you can schedule time to review your essay drafts or simply study with a peer tutor who already got an A- or higher in the class you're taking.

You will feel supported

One of my classmates started losing motivation after leaving the track team and started to procrastinate. Eventually, he was failing his classes. Harvard worked with him to have him take some time off to work and mature and then come back to finish his studies.

The best in academia

Beyond your career success, going to an Ivy means that you get to attend one of the oldest education institutions in the US. In fact,

Future Ivy

Harvard was the first higher education institution in the US, created in 1636.[6] The other Ivies were founded in the 18th century.

This means you are reminded of great scholars who have attended before you, like Ralph Waldo Emerson (who has the philosophy building named after him), or the original psychologist William James, who enrolled in 1861 and was an influential psychology scholar (and whose name now rests on the Harvard psychology building).[7]

I remember in one government class, we were debating what one of the leading political scholars meant in his writing.

My teacher said, "You can go ask him. He's right down the hall."

I was shocked. I realized that a lot of the top influential political scholars were in the same building as my class. This is not only the case for government majors but also economics, psychology, and many more.

Going to an Ivy means you get access to these leaders in the field and will be surrounded by a place that has held the highest standards of pedagogy, education, academia, and the pursuit of knowledge for centuries!

---

[6] https://www.bestcolleges.com/blog/history-of-ivy-league/

[7] https://psychology.fas.harvard.edu/people/william-james

Summary

* In this chapter, you learned some of the reasons it's beneficial to go to an Ivy League school.
* Whether it's the abundance of resources, financial aid, world class teachers, amazing classmates, or incredible professional network, going to a top school has lifetime benefits that will help you find jobs easier and accelerate your career.

Action Steps

- Reflect on how you think the Ivy League could help you in your career. Are you planning to go to grad school?

Future Ivy

CHAPTER 3

α

Be different

We all have this in common — we are masters at comparing ourselves to others. We get upset when our peers do better than we do. We scheme how we can make up the difference and be better. Sometimes, we let the envy and jealousy sink into our souls and demotivate us. Comparison and imitation does one thing. It makes you another admission package waiting to be rejected from a top school.

Imagine, though, if you stopped yourself more often. You could find activities that you actually enjoy and revel in. You could stop the endless jealousy and chart your own path. You could become a world-class writer or a famous comedian. The possibilities are limitless. You become limitless.

Fitting in is addictive

There are no uncomfortable questions when you fit in. People approve of you. You are the status quo. You have friends who are just like you and share common interests. It feels good to belong.

To be different, you won't feel like you belong. You will feel like a loner, and it can suck. We want to fit in because social rejection hurts. Studies show that the brain feels rejection similarly to physical pain.[8]

---

[8] https://www.pnas.org/content/pnas/108/15/6270.full.pdf

I've dealt with that pain. I didn't have a lot of friends in high school and sometimes wondered what it would be like to be a "normal" high school student — hanging out in a clique, gossiping about cute boys, and obsessing over prom.

I got over it by reminding myself why I was doing it. Your "why" is your secret reserve. It's the fuel that keeps you going when you are drained. Your why needs to be charged emotionally. It needs to bring you to tears (if crying comes easily).

For me, it was all about creating a better life for my future family. I grew up in a chaotic household full of fighting, violence, and hatred. I not only wanted to get out, but I wanted to help others escape and create a better life for themselves, too.

Find your escape

Your escape is something that literally takes you away from your worries. It's an activity that gives you energy and doesn't drain you. It's an activity that lights you up and makes you lose track of time.

It's an effort that gives back to the community and makes the world a better place. If you can't think of one, that's okay. You can develop this over time.

For me, it was teaching. I loved that lightbulb moment when a student I was tutoring just got it. Sometimes, it would be a basic math problem that I explained in four different ways before they understood. I loved teaching public speaking and debate. These are skills that give you a voice, the confidence to make change, and a platform to get noticed.

In my chaotic family, I didn't feel like I had a voice that mattered, so speech and debate filled that void.

The work never ends

The good thing is, if you find your escape, it will feel less like work and you will feel more energized to do it.

Fitting in is always going to haunt you. People will expect you to do what everyone else is doing and resisting this can be exhausting. The work of being different never ends.

If you do the work, you will stand out

This is where your "why" comes into play. Make it a strong enough "why" that it keeps the fire hot.

If your mission is to inspire teens and young adults to find their voice, pick someone specific in the group to focus on. Your cousin, your sister, someone you can visualize. Imagine how your activity will help them. It will give them the confidence to stand up to bullies. It will give them the confidence to speak out against bad managers. It will give them the confidence to pursue what they want vs. what others want.

In a world where everyone is copying each other's next moves, you can stand out by being different.

There is no better time to start than now. The better you get at being different, the more you'll stand out, be admitted to good schools, and most importantly, move toward being the person you actually want to be.

Why does this matter?

You will be constantly bombarded with tales of what everyone else is doing — the social media feeds, the parents, the gossiping grandmas. You will be tempted to follow in your older siblings' paths.

When you fall into that temptation, you will be living every life besides your own. You deserve to live your own life, develop your own passion, and achieve your own dreams.

However, these opportunities aren't going to show up on their own. If they did, the rest of your classmates would be taking advantage of them. You need to scavenge and sometimes even build them yourself.

What you really need to do

It revolves around the two-word mentality: Be Different. Do things that other students and even adults would question your ability to do at your age. For example, I got my first job at 14. My classmates asked, "Are we even allowed to get a job this young?" I answered, "Yes, you can get a work permit at 14, or even younger in some fields." I had googled it, of course.

What actually happened was that I unknowingly created my own internship. While visiting my high school's career office, I mentioned to my counselor, Mrs. K, that I was really passionate about working in Law, and she referred me to a local Law office that needed help filing documents and helping lawyers. Boom. Paid internship.

You need to resist other people's opinions. You need to stop doing what your parents suggest, just because all the other kids are doing it — like the volunteer trips that my grandmother thought I should take because the other neighborhood kids were doing them.

You should stop joining clubs just because your friends are doing it. For example, the honor society, academic decathlon, and journalism. Stop all the nonsense activities that you are doing just to have an "accomplished" resume. Decide that you want to be different.

Future Ivy

Summary

- In this chapter, you learned that comparing yourself to others is not only common but a default that we must break in order to be true to ourselves.
- There are countless other students who want to get into the Ivy League, so you have to adopt a mentality of "being different" to make sure the admissions officers remember you.
- One way to be different is by going all-in on the activities that inspire you most and resisting other people's opinions.

Action Steps

- ☐ Brainstorm your "why" by asking questions like: if money was no object, what would I be doing right now? Which activities that I'm a part of utilize my strengths to their fullest? What are some topics or careers that I'm deeply curious about?

CHAPTER 4

α

How to stay motivated

The cops knew our house well. After the 2001 telecom recession, my family fought non-stop about money. It sometimes ended with the cops knocking on the front door of our house.

"Stop crying, kid. Be calm like your sister," the police officer said to me. But how could I stay calm in a house that was full of such financial distress? They didn't have an answer for me, so I channeled all my energy into creating a better life for my future family.

The only way I believed I could have a better life was by getting into the best college possible. I set my sights on the Ivies, hoping to get as far away from my chaotic family in California as I could. The stakes were high, too. My parents couldn't afford to pay for my college, so I would need to get a full-ride scholarship in order to make it happen.

Thus, I spent every waking second strategizing as to how I could stand out to the Ivy League and not get distracted by all the fighting and divisions in my home. The first thing I did was get over-the-ear headphones to block out all the arguments. Then I removed the TV from my room, filled out my planner every day, and got access to the library at the local community college near my home by doing dual enrollment (which is when you take college classes while in high school).

It was a grind

Future Ivy

I took almost every one of the hardest classes available at my school, pursued internships, and took on leadership positions. My schedule looked like this every single day:

> 7am: wake up, drink coffee, get to school
> 7:30-3pm: attend school
> 3-6pm: cross-country practice
> 6-7pm: get home and eat 3 bowls of rice (seriously!)
> 7-8pm: math homework
> 8-9pm: science homework
> 9-10pm: English homework
> 10-11pm: study Spanish
> 11pm: shower, attempt to go to bed with wet hair, get scolded by grandma to dry it
> 11:30pm: zzzzzzz

In senior year, I spent 2+ hours per day taking ACT practice tests, because I wasn't a natural test taker, and it paid off. I increased my score from 30 to 34 (the highest score you can get is a 36), which is good enough for the top schools.

After I applied for colleges, I spent hours every day applying for local, state, and national scholarships, as I knew I would have to support myself through school. This also paid off, and I got a full ride to any college I wanted (Thanks to the Bill and Melinda Gates Foundation!).[9]

You get through the grind by having a "why." My "why" was to work hard now so that I would have an easier future and less struggles with money than my family did. Your "why" might be that you lost a

---

[9] https://www.thegatesscholarship.org/scholarship

friend to cancer and you want to fundraise to invest more money into research for a cure. Or maybe your "why" is that you love animals and think they should be treated better and have more rights. Or maybe you see how hard your family works and you want to be able to provide them with a better quality of life.

Your source of motivation

Who do you think will succeed more? Bob, who wants to be a doctor only for the money, or Sally, who wants to be a doctor so that people like her dad, who struggles with diabetes, live healthier and longer lives? Who is more likely to keep going after a terrible organic chemistry exam?

If you answered Sally, you are onto something. Your "why" is your secret reserve of energy. It's the fuel that keeps you going after all that AP/IB, advanced class homework. Not all "whys" are equal; a purpose-driven one like Sally's is premium-grade fuel.

It keeps you going, even though you may be in quarantine and stuck inside and not able to see your friends. It keeps you going, even though you think you suck at physics and think it's too hard for you. It keeps you going, even though people tell you that they don't believe you could get into an Ivy or that you dream too big (there will be haters on your journey, and you can prove them wrong!).

Your "why" might be about creating a better life for your future family, or maybe it's about developing mentorship for women in STEM, so that female voices and experiences are better represented in those disciplines (Did you know that there are no crash test dummies that represent the average women in vehicle safety tests? That's just one reason we need more females in STEM!).[10]

If you do the work, you will stand out. This is where your "why" comes into play. Make it a strong "why" that keeps the fire hot. If your mission is to inspire teens and young adults to find their voice, pick someone specific in that group to focus on. For example, you could picture hosting a public speaking class to 8th-graders, and it ends up giving confidence to Tina, who goes on to lead social justice movements. Or maybe you help your cousin stand up to bullies and now you want to work on cyberbullying policies.

Imagine how your activity will help those you care about. Visualizing the benefits of your work will help keep you motivated.

There is no better time than now to find your "why." The more you stay motivated, the more you'll stand out. The more you stand out, the likelier you are to be admitted to the top schools you've chosen.

The nosy 5-year-old test

To figure out your "why," do the "nosy 5-year-old sister test." Pretend you have a little sister, and she can't stop asking you why. Every time you talk to her, she asks you, "Why?" five times.

"I'm going out," you say.

"Why?" she asks.

"I have to go to the store," you reply.

Why?" she insists.

---

[10] https://www.discovermagazine.com/technology/why-are-there-no-crash-test-dummies-that-represent-average-women

"To get milk and sugar," you respond.

"Why?" she inquires.

"So I can make a cake," you answer.

"Why?" she asks again.

"Because the store-bought cakes have too much icing," you retort.

"Why?" she questions.

"Because it's mom's birthday tomorrow, and she likes my homemade cakes," you admit.

By asking "why" five times, your little sister found the real reason you wanted to go to the store. You can use the same principle to discover the reason you will continue to persevere.

If you aren't sure of your "why," which is totally normal, you can reflect on this question: Why do you get up in the morning? Besides the delicious coffee or hot chocolate that your mom makes you in the morning, it may be that you are excited to work or learn more about animal rights, or that you want to run a better race every day, or learn new languages.

For example, Sally is interested in learning languages. To find her motivation, we can ask her "Why?" 5x.

(1)   *Why are you interested in learning languages?*

Sally: I feel that in order to understand a culture, you need to learn the language.

(2)   *Why is it important for you to understand cultures?*

Sally: Understanding someone's culture helps you connect with other humans.

(3)   *Why is it important to connect with other humans?*

Sally: We are so connected with our technology but not connected by being present and making people feel heard.

(4)   *Why is it important for people to feel heard?*

Sally: Being heard is the first step to solving problems and gathering information.

(5)   *Why is it important to solve problems?*

Sally: My parents had a lot of problems in their marriage. They didn't know how or even want to problem-solve, and then they ended up getting divorced. I want to be someone who sticks it out and is part of the solution.

Here, you see Sally's true motivation for wanting to be someone who sticks it out and is a problem solver, because of her upbringing. How has your upbringing influenced your motivation?

For me, I struggled a lot with money chaos when I was growing up and know how much that can harm our relationships. That's why I was motivated to become highly employable by attending the best colleges, and that's why I'm teaching you how to stand out to these top schools.

I want you to be highly employable so that you don't have to worry about getting a job or paying for your next utility bill, so that you can focus on developing loving relationships.

Summary

* In this chapter you learned that getting into the Ivy League is tough.
* From keeping up your grades, working with teachers, serving in after school clubs, getting internships, and studying for the ACT, your life has to be organized, and you have to be disciplined.
* You also learned that all this energy doesn't just appear, you have to create it by having a strong reason underneath it all, by having a strong, personal "why."
* You can start to figure out your "why" by using the "nosy 5-year-old test."

Action Steps

- ☐ Start brainstorming your "why" by asking yourself "Why?" 5x
- ☐ Write down your "why" and put it somewhere you can see it every day, like a post-it note on your mirror.

CHAPTER 5

α

How to stand out to the Ivy League with the ACHIEVE system

After the last chapters, you now understand that you can't be doing all the activities everyone else is doing. Instead, you have to be different. However, you need to balance this with advanced classes and test prep and understand that at times, it will be difficult to figure out what to prioritize.

Back to this "being different" part. You may still be wondering, "How am I supposed to be different?" Well, you can be different by showing tremendous effort and getting to know your teachers. These are key people at school who can help you get into advanced classes if you're not already in them, pass with flying colors, and get glowing letters of recommendation for college. Then, you can work on finding a mentor for your career search. These are people who care about your development and can help you land internships as well as help you practice informational interviewing.

Yes. This is in fact a lot of information, a lot of steps, and a lot of people to get a hold of. Luckily, you picked up this book, and I'm about to help you remember all these things in order with one word: ACHIEVE.

Whenever you get lost or need to know the next step, you can follow the ACHIEVE system. 7 baby steps to finding your stand-out factor. The system is made to be followed in order, so that you know how to prioritize your time. Even though you could do two steps at once, it's less stressful and less overwhelming if you finish step 1 before going on to step 2, etc. I recommend that you only focus on one step at a time. Once you get good at that step, then you can move on to conquering the next level.

Before the standout system

Before I learned about having an application theme or spike or niche, I struggled to pick extracurriculars, figure out if I was on the right track, and how to stand out in a sea of applicants, especially other Asians with amazing stats.

I felt lost and didn't think I was unique enough for the Ivy League. I wasn't able to prioritize or see a path to getting into those top colleges.

Things were hard because my immigrant family had high expectations for me as the oldest child, and I didn't want to disappoint them. It was difficult, because they would constantly bring up the achievements of other kids, like Julie's daughter, who just got into Harvard, or Sunny's son, who got a national award for piano. Does this sound familiar?

But now, I want you to imagine what your life could be like. Ever since I implemented the ACHIEVE system, I was able to feel like I was on the right track, feel less confused about my future, and feel confident that I was going to stand out to the top schools. Because of that, I was able to get into my dream school, Harvard, and got accepted at other notable schools like UC Berkeley, Dartmouth, and Duke. I was so excited about this that I shared it with a student who also used the system and got into Harvard early action.

This standout system works for international students too

One student I coached was an international student who was worried about extracurriculars, since her school didn't have clubs. After putting the ACHIEVE plan into action, she had opportunities coming in from all over the place, like a rocket science internship and other research opportunities. She no doubt will be a standout applicant to top schools. Can you imagine what that would be like?

I want you to know something about me. I'm not a superhero with special gifts or talents. I actually still struggle to understand what makes me different and unique. And that's what I love about this system - I don't have to worry about that anymore!

I'm going to take you step by step through a system I've developed over years of evaluating my process, coaching students, and researching other Ivy League student admission journeys.

There are 7 steps and corresponding skills you need to master in order to stand out

In the following chapters, I'll walk you through each step and give you examples to see it in action. In brackets is an associated skill for that step.

1. A: As in advanced classes (The 4-year Advanced Schedule)
2. C: Conduct an activity audit (The Time Audit)
3. H: Help your teacher help you (The Avocado Toast Method)
4. I: Ignite your interests (Online Outreach)
5. E: Execute your theme (Finding your Theme)
6. V: Validate your credibility (Resume Writing for Impact)
7. E: Earn your SAT/ACT exams score (The Accountability Buddy)

Future Ivy

You can use the acronym "ACHIEVE" to easily remember the steps, in order. In the following chapters, you'll learn about each step in depth and how to apply it to your own plan. Every chapter will have examples from different majors that will help you apply it to your own goals.

Summary

* In this chapter you were introduced to the concept of ACHIEVE, a system that will help you figure out where you are in the application process and provide skills to help you finish your college application like a boss.
* The ACHIEVE system has been proven with students from all backgrounds and will be your ultimate checklist for success.

Action Steps

- [ ] Write down what each letter of the ACHIEVE system means
- [ ] Reflect on where you stand with respect to each one

Future Ivy

Part 2

β

The ACHIEVE System

Future Ivy

CHAPTER 6

β

Step 1 of Achieve – Aim for As in advanced classes

In an acronym, each individual letter can help you remember a larger concept. The "A" in ACHIEVE stands for "Aim for As in Advanced Classes"

Let's break it down one baby step at a time. Why do you need to take advanced classes? And sure, "easier said than done," right? There's actually a loophole here. Advanced class just means a subject that most interests you and pushes you to learn more. Think about it: you probably don't need to try that hard in your favorite class, because it feels fun AND you end up with better grades than in your most loathsome subjects. The bottom line is, if you really like a subject, it's going to be easier to get As in those classes and you should go all-in.

Take classes you find interesting

You've probably experienced it when reading about certain topics makes time go by in a blur. One minute, you're reading about something you find super interesting… and the next minute, an hour has gone by.

You may also have been so bored reading something so uninteresting that you were on the verge of falling asleep, slamming your head onto a book, and getting the whole class to laugh at you. The point is, nobody can trick you into getting good grades in classes you are just not interested in.

You still need good grades in the core subjects, such as English and the sciences, and you should take the top-level classes of all the courses offered at your high school, partly because it shows a rigorous schedule and partly to expose you to different types of thinking and subjects.

Striving for a rigorous class schedule is also a great way of showing the Ivy League admissions officer that you are the kind of student who can handle multiple deadlines and high pressure and showcase your dedication to a specific career track.

While it's important to shine in your best classes, you also need to consider the overall rigor of your program by looking at your friend's classes. I recommend you talk to your guidance counselor to confirm first-hand the "rigor" of your school's classes. You want to make sure your schedule is considered "most rigorous" by your guidance counselor.

Basically, if all the advanced students at your school are taking 10 AP classes, then you really need to be meeting that average plus or minus 1. It's not a perfect measurement, but you have to at least meet the standards at your own school, because your application will be directly compared first with students at your own and neighboring schools.

Getting into advanced classes

It was a shock to many people in my community when they found out I got into Harvard because I was never that "smart kid." Starting in 3rd grade, they gave us an assessment to identify the gifted students, and, hint, hint: I was not one of them. I remember then in 4th grade the kids labeled "gifted" would leave to do their advanced curriculum while I stayed behind with the other normal kids.

Because I was not in the gifted program in elementary school, I was not placed in advanced classes in middle school (I know, it's crazy how young this starts). This meant that in 7th grade, I was in a regular English class, not honors, and not the most advanced math class. At the time, it didn't really concern me, because I never realized there was even a difference.

In English class, I did my best in class by doing all my homework, participating in class, and staying during break to ask questions. In 7th grade, my English teacher recommended that I try for the honors English class, so I opted in to the assessment.

It was a weird exam that had puzzles related to every question, with multiple choice pattern recognition and spatial intelligence tests. For example, there was a 5-by-5 grid, and each of the squares had one heart, star, or circle. You had to figure out the pattern to fill in the last empty square.

I struggled with every question, and in the end I felt like I had guessed on all of them. When I went home, I was frustrated. I wondered, "How do shapes relate to English? Did this test really measure my intelligence?" Unsurprisingly, a few months later I found out that I had failed!

Luckily, my English teacher had seen the hard work that I put into the class by asking tons of questions and staying during breaks, and I had been given such a wonderful recommendation that they decided to let me into the more advanced class anyway. The point of the story is that so-called "intelligence tests" are not an accurate measurement of your potential but unfortunately bear a lot of weight in your academic future. The real key is getting your teachers to help you into the advanced classes.

Future Ivy

Another example is with my math class. Because I hadn't passed those intelligence tests, I also had to start in a lower-level math class, and to make matters worse, on the first day of my 7th grade class, I remember the teacher called out all the names of all the people who had forgotten to write their last names on their assignments, since it wasn't elementary school anymore.

"Amy! your last name isn't on the paper. Amy who? You need to put your last name on your papers in middle school," my math teacher scolded me in front of the class.

I dug my chin into my sweater and hoped there was another Amy in the class who she was talking to and that she wouldn't realize it was me. I was scared that this rough start would jeopardize my chances of getting into a good college. I wasn't the only one. Everyone was terrified of her after that.

Later on, though, I was struggling on a math assignment and needed help. I couldn't or didn't want to ask my dad, because the last time I asked for help, in 4th grade, he solved the math problem in seconds without explaining any of the steps. My dad is super smart and won lots of academic competitions in China, but he wasn't the best at explaining things, since the rest of us non-geniuses are slower and need to figure things out step-by-step.

Back in school, I mustered the courage to ask my math teacher for help after class. I remember walking up the ramp to her brown shipping container classroom. When I opened the door, the smell of fresh paint and old papers embraced me. I made eye contact with my math teacher, who was grading alone.

A ball of crumpled paper seemed to pass in front of us in the awkward silence. I finally said that I had some questions about the assignment.

Like the skies parting after a biblical flood, her face lit up, and she said, "That's what I'm here for, honey, to help you learn this!"

And she did! She turned out to be a sweet woman and showed me dozens of pictures of her nieces and nephews. I went back several times to make sure I was understanding the concepts correctly. In one of our after school meetings, she told me that I might be a good fit for the more advanced math class. She said, "I don't want to see you go, but since you are such a great student, I want you to be more challenged. I will check on the other class for you." She did, and I got into the advanced math class, Algebra 2 honors, in 7th grade.

Your teachers are an important resource

The key point is to spend time with your teachers, help them understand what your goals are. If you do the work and show initiative to master the topics, teachers will more than likely recommend you for higher-level classes. Start by going to your teacher's office hours and asking for help. You'll be surprised how much they want to assist you. If you are nervous, you can recruit a friend to come with you.

Your guidance counselor

Another important resource is your guidance counselor. I remember signing up for one of the spots to talk about my class schedule, even though I felt like a small fish in a big pond (I went to a big public high school, so there were about 400 students per counselor).

Future Ivy

I know it can feel like they are too busy and don't want to be bothered, but that's their job! They're there to help you in your academic, career, and college plans. I was introduced to the counselor when he came to one of my 9th grade classes and made a presentation about how to use the counselor office and create a 4-year class plan. I took a chance on that offer and signed up for a time to create my 4-year plan.

When I arrived at the counselor's office, it was eerily quiet. I had expected lines of students, but there were none today. I was glad but also wondered whether this was a good sign. I walked in and was greeted by a cheerful Mr. Sklove, the guidance counselor for last names starting from C to J.

He was warm and really made me feel comfortable. He had many posters of the marathons he'd run and some of the bands that he liked. We got to know each other and got down to business. We worked together on a rigorous 4-year schedule that included some classes at the local community college through a program called dual enrollment. We also worked out a schedule where I could participate in the community college debate team, since our high school didn't have one (debate was important for me), which normally met 1:30pm-4:30pm 2 times per week. My counselor helped me approach my senior year teachers to make sure I was off school by 12:00pm and could make the debate team at the local community college. It was great!

Your counselor and teachers joined their profession to help you grow. I interviewed my high school counselor for this book and he said, "The main reason I'm here is to support the students. I wish more students came in with their questions." Take advantage of your high school counseling department, especially during a non-busy period when you can get to know them on a personal level. I am a firm believer that you can achieve anything with the right help, so get to know your counselors and teachers and wow them with your determination and initiative.

When I was in junior high, I was not originally in the most advanced classes. I wanted a bigger challenge, so I took placement tests and worked with my teachers and guidance counselor to show initiative. By making a good impression on my teachers, I was able to get the recommendation that boosted my placement test results enough to get me into the most advanced classes.

What's more important to note is that by doing this, you will be building your network! Teachers went into this profession to help students just like you. Building your network will help you later on down the line when you want to start a club and need a teacher as the club advisor or need a classroom in which to meet. It can help you get opportunities that no other students have heard of, like the ability to represent the school at the UC Berkeley young workers' rights summit. It can help you get the stellar letters of recommendation that help humanize you in the admissions process.

What if you aren't good at talking to adults?

It's normal to be intimidated by adults, and two things can help you get past this fear. The first is to be prepared with questions. The first time I met with my guidance counselor, I brought a list of questions, like how can I create an advanced schedule without overwhelming myself, and what clubs would be good to explore if I'm interested in law and medicine? For my initial experiences going into my teachers' break time, I would bring a problem or two that I was struggling with. Being prepared can help with your nerves.

The second thing is to slow down your breathing. Your brain collects data on how your body is feeling, so if your heart starts racing, then your brain might start panicking and you might faint. 4-7-8 breathing is a great technique to use before approaching your teachers or even before giving a talk. To do it, you breathe in for 4 seconds, hold for 7, and then exhale for 8. Then repeat 10x. This will help decrease your heart rate so you can speak normally to your teachers.

Skill: The 4-year advanced schedule

Getting an advanced schedule - your plan

The 4-year advanced schedule is your master plan and timeline. It will be shortened depending on how long you have left in high school. This is the document that you'll refer to again and again and will help make a lot of conversations much easier to start, such as helping your teachers understand why you need to take a certain advanced class. In your 4-year plan you can also figure out with your counselor how to find more classes related to your interests and even find internships.

First, meet with your counselor, preferably when it's not the busy season finalizing classes. Create a 4-year class plan with advanced classes and electives you are excited about. Then adjust each year.

If you weren't already in advanced classes and you are ready for a bigger challenge, you can use the 4-year advanced schedule to advocate for yourself in school in three ways:

1) Ask the advanced class teacher for a spot. In school, you have two main guides. The first is your high school counselor and the second

is the teacher of your advanced classes. Get to know them both and share your desire for a bigger challenge.

2) Explore alternatives like dual enrollment at the local community college or online class sites like APEX. One of my students uses APEX to take AP classes that don't fit in her schedule or that her school doesn't offer. You can also self-study for AP exams with resources like UC Scout.

3) Take a placement test. Some schools are open access, meaning you can choose whatever classes you want, and some will require you to take a test to qualify for an advanced class.

When I interviewed my high school counselor, he told me a story about a student who wanted to get into an advanced math class, but the advanced math teacher didn't believe he was ready, since he had received a B in his last math class. My counselor recommended that he take the placement test at the community college. He did, and he did well enough in the community college class to get into an even more advanced math class in high school the next year.

Don't let anyone stop you, whether that be a teacher, family member, or negative friends. There are often alternative paths to your goal.

Aiming for As

Now that you've learned how to get into an advanced class, I have some tips to not just survive but thrive. Many students ask me if it's better to get an A in a regular class or a B in an advanced class. That is not the best question if you want to get into a top school, where all your peers are definitely taking advanced classes. You already know it's better to take advanced classes, so a better question to ask is, how do you get an A in advanced classes?

In freshman year of honors English, my teacher announced that we were going to have a test on the *Odyssey,* and I panicked because I hadn't read a single page (I hated assigned reading and relied heavily on summary sites like Sparknotes and Shmoop). I went home and tried to make sense of the old translated stories but quickly fell asleep.

"Ah man, I'm never going to get through this," I said to myself after flipping through the hundreds of boring pages left in the book.

Then I thought, maybe I can study for this test by quizzing myself with a bunch of online quizzes. I quickly googled "Odyssey book test," and to my surprise, I found tons of quizzes and even a 100-question practice test. I first started on Quizlet to work my way through themes and character descriptions, then I found some other quizzes about the plot. Pretty soon, I felt ready to take a 100-question test and got a solid 85 without even reading the book! I did make note of all the questions I got wrong and went back through those descriptions to make sure I found the right answer.

The next day, I had my exam. I was nervous as my English teacher passed out the exams.

"Exams face down until I say so," my English teacher, with short gray hair and glasses with no frames, said. "Okay, you can start the exam! Keep your eyes on your own paper."

I anxiously turned over the exam and contemplated my fate for the next hour. I was stunned. I feverishly flipped through the 100 questions and realized that this was the exact same test I'd taken online.

Jackpot. Needless to say, the test was super easy, and I was out of there in record time looking like a boss.

After this exam, I learned that finding quizzes online to reinforce your knowledge could really help you ace your next exam. Also there are certain ways of studying for tests that are more effective than others. For example, flashcard and memory devices like mnemonics work great for classes with lots of terminology. I still remember the taxonomy rank from 7th grade science class because of this mnemonic: Kings Play Chess On Flat Green Squares (kingdom, phylum, class, order, family, genus, and species). Another thing you can do is set things to song. For example, I still remember the US presidents' names in order from 8th grade history class because our teacher had us recite it to Yankee Doodle's tune. Get creative and make the studying fun for you!

Learning styles

Everyone's a little different with their learning styles. For me, I learn by doing. I remember sitting in one of my Calculus classes and thinking I have no clue what my math teacher is saying. My math teacher was one of the best in the school, but I'm not a visual or auditory learner. I learn by doing, meaning that I learn by doing the math problems, testing myself with online quizzes, and using flashcards.

You can make your studying much more efficient once you find your learning style. There are 4 types of learning styles and they form the acronym VARK: visual, auditory, reading/writing, and kinesthetic.[11]

Visual learners do well when they use charts and diagrams in their studying. Auditory learners do well when they hear the material recited

---

[11] https://educationonline.ku.edu/community/4-different-learning-styles-to-know

to them, like in a lecture. Reading and writing oriented learners benefit from taking notes and reviewing slides. Kinesthetic learners like me do well by engaging their senses by using flashcards to study or with hands-on learning like in a science lab. To figure out your style, you can reflect on what's worked for you and experiment in your next exam study session with flashcards, YouTube videos, creating word mnemonics like PEMDAS, or songs. Mix it up and find what works best.

Your syllabus

Your playbook to good grades is your syllabus, so you should read through it to understand the rules of the game. It might say that 80% of the grade is determined by tests and quizzes and 20% is determined by homework. If I were you, I would hone my test-taking skills by studying the tests. My mentality on the first exam is to understand the types of questions that will be on the next exam. With each test, you can get better at predicting what's going to be on the exams and how you can study for them in your learning style.

Your syllabus might also reveal your ability to get a grade buffer, a.k.a extra credit. But more important are the dates on the syllabus for the exams. Create reminders to start studying for an exam a full week early, so you have time for the knowledge to soak in and you are less anxious about having to cram. Google Calendar is great for setting up alerts on your phone so you can prevent cramming for exams.

After you've studied your syllabus and put calendar reminders for the big test dates, create ways for you to check on your grade progress. Just like a roof leak is better to be detected earlier rather than later, keeping tabs on your grades can help you reach higher grades, since you will know sooner if they are slipping and can change your behavior.

Your cure for a slipping grade

1) Make sure you turn in any missing or lost assignments. Some points are better than none, plus sometimes things get lost even if you've turned it in.
2) Start attending the teacher's office hours at least every other week.
3) Monitor your grades.

Getting to know your teachers and getting help on your homework will help increase your understanding of the material. This also helps the teacher learn more about your character and your resourcefulness, which are all amazing if you want a great recommendation letter. You can review essays, feedback, or exams that will help you tailor your studying to what's going to be on the test.

Sometimes teachers will post your grades, but sometimes you are on your own, so you need to take the initiative to ask your teacher once in a while - no more than once every two months, or you'll be seen as a grade grubber, which admissions hates.

You can create your own record of your grades so that when progress reports come, you have your own record of what assignments you turned in and the scores you received on exams. You'd be surprised how many errors can happen due to simple human mistakes.

ACHIEVE in action - English example

Imagine that you grow up with your father and mother reading the New York Times every single morning. You become fascinated by the international section and always ask your parents to help you understand it. You are not sure what your career will be but you love English, so you decide to pursue a bachelor's in English. You know there are lots of great writers that apply to top schools, so you use the ACHIEVE system to make sure that you are standing out.

Step 1 - Aim for As in Advanced Classes

You feel good about step one. You are taking all the AP classes, getting good grades, and you've even decided to take some non-fiction writing classes at your local community college.

Step 2 - Conduct an Activity Audit

In step two, you realize that there are three activities you no longer enjoy that take up a lot of time. For example, you used to love playing volleyball; however, since your injury, you've decided that yoga is a better fit. Also, in ninth grade you struggled in math, so your parents had you go to a math tutoring center, but you figured out how to study math on your own and no longer need it. You also used to love doing debate and you still do, but you feel comfortable enough with public speaking and want more time to write. You make the hard but right decision to cut those activities.

Step 3 - Help your Teacher Help You

In step three, you start going to your English teacher's office hours. You find out that she really wants to start a student newspaper but hasn't found the right student to lead this. You tell her that you're up for this and you work with your counselor to get this established as a real club.

Step 4 - Ignite your Interests

Next, you reach out to your role models in the non-fiction space, like the journalists who write in the papers your parents read. You make sure that you are actively supporting them on social media, and after four months of persistence, you get an informational interview from one of these journalists.

Step 5 - Execute your Theme

You also start writing daily for the newspaper, so you can practice your writing craft. After your informational interview with the journalist, you keep in touch so that one day they can serve as your mentor. You continue to support their work and send them celebratory emails when one of their articles gets serious exposure.

Step 6 - Validate your Credibility

Meanwhile, you are researching writing competitions, and you enter all of the non-fiction ones. Before submitting your essays, you get some feedback from your English teacher and your mentor. You end up winning one of the competitions hosted by the foreign services and you win a trip to DC.

Your mentor happens to be in DC, so you arrange a coffee meeting to get to know each other in person. Your mentor offers you an opportunity to help contribute to a big article. You gladly accept, and once the article is published, you save it to include in your college application supplementary materials.

Step 7 - Earn your Target SAT / ACT score

Toward the end of junior year, you decide to take the SAT and you find a study buddy to help you drill the exams every weekend. After 50 practice tests, you get your target score of 1550 out of 1600.

Future Ivy

You are admitted to Stanford, UPenn, and many other great schools!

Summary

* In step 1 of ACHIEVE, you learned the importance of getting into the most advanced classes that your school has to offer.
* You learned some of the main ways to get your teachers and counselors to help you in this process, and it all starts with creating a 4-year plan.
* Finally, you learned some tips to do well in your classes and earn your As.

Action Steps

☐ Get into the most advanced classes at your school
☐ Get As in most classes
☐ Create a 4-year plan with your counselor

CHAPTER 7

β

Step 2 of Achieve - Conduct an Activity Audit

Now that you've focused on creating good study habits to score As in your advanced classes, let's dive into the biggest thing that holds students back from standing out: your lack of free time. It may be surprising how many activities we accumulate when we go through our list, kind of like how when you move you are surprised by how much stuff you have.

Here's my own list of activities for Junior year:

- School Newspaper Club
- Academic Decathlon
- Key Club community service
- National Honor Society
- Cross-country
- Youth Commission
- Health Occupation Students of America
- Volunteering with disabled kids at Giant Steps Therapy
- Debate Club
- Internships

None of these activities are inherently bad, of course. However, with too much on our plate, we lose focus. Doing one thing well allows us to go deep, as opposed to swimming in the shallow end by trying to tackle everything. If you need more help with this, a good book about how less is better is called *Essentialism: The Disciplined Pursuit of Less* by

Greg McKeown. When I got serious about going to Harvard, I knew I had to seriously cut activities and focus. I decided to focus on debate and internships. This worked out well for me, but the key is that I focused on a few projects and was able to learn way more and have more impact.

I know it's not easy. Some friends will pressure you to join their clubs and classes. You want to spend time with them, but know it's not the right fit. Your parents will tell you about a volunteer trip that all the other kids are going on. You don't want to disappoint your parents, but you know it's not right for your schedule. Your English teacher will encourage you to join the high-school newspaper. You hate writing but think it will look good on your resume. Say to all of them, "Thank you, but it's not for me."

Start thinking about all the activities that take up your time. Better yet, write them down. Go through each activity. Is this a "hell-yes" activity (as in, do you enjoy it and does the activity make you into the person you want to be)? If not, consider cutting it. Is cross-country worth all your evenings? Does it bring joy to your heart? If not, Marie Kondo it.

We often have activities that outlive their purpose. I started running in ninth grade as a way to spend time with my best friend. She moved away at the end of the year, but I continued running. In eleventh grade, I realized I didn't enjoy running, so I cut it. If you really want to stand out, you need to learn how to manage your time like a pro. It's easy to see the reasons the students that come to me for coaching have such a hard time standing out. Keep in mind that these are the highest achieving kids in their groups.

So, why do they struggle standing out? It's because they are so busy! Think about it; they're doing the homework for their advanced classes and SAT prep, while also trying to keep up with community service, school clubs, and family responsibilities. These students don't have the time to craft personal projects or pursue passions that make them stand out amongst other top students.

Skill: The Time Audit

The key is called an "Activity Audit"

How are you spending most of your time? Instead of wondering where it all went, let's be strategic with your time. Write down all the activities that take up your time and be as detailed as possible. I discovered that I was spending most of my time in lectures and doing homework for the many AP classes I was taking. Now ask yourself: Do you really enjoy this activity or subject? Does it fit in with what you want to do in the future?

At that time, I realized that I rarely retained facts from lectures. This wasn't my fault or the teacher's fault. I went to a big public school with a strong faculty. It was just about my learning style. I don't learn well by passively watching and listening but rather by doing and practicing. This means that I would spend an hour in math class and feel like I hadn't learned anything. I found that doing the example problems on my own helped me learn in 20 minutes what I was struggling to retain from the hour-long lectures. Figure out how you learn best by reflecting and taking learning style tests online.

This realization led me to take more independent study classes and feel okay missing lectures for my extracurriculars (I traveled a lot for debate). I took classes at the local community college because they were more self-guided and fit my learning style better. Additionally, one summer semester there counted toward a full academic year at my high school, so I was able to free up a lot of time during my normal school schedule.

Talk to your high school counselor to see if there are similar programs, AKA dual enrollment, with your local community college or university.

How to do a "Class Time Audit"

I usually recommend taking the most challenging classes available like honors, IB, or AP. However, it is completely okay to opt for an easier AP or even regular class if it's not a core course or related to your career goal.

Core classes include: English, Math, Foreign Language, and Sciences, so take the harder classes of those. Keep in mind that top schools like the Ivy League want to see 3+ years of a foreign language in high school. If languages are not a big focus for you, take the less time-consuming languages, like Spanish, instead of Chinese.

When choosing classes, be mindful of how much time they will take. You can ask teachers and upperclassmen for their opinion. For instance, at my school, AP Statistics was known to be less time consuming than AP Calculus BC, so if your future career goal does not emphasize hard maths, then take AP Stats.

If your career goal is to be a doctor, you should take the harder science classes, like AP Biology or Chemistry. In this case, you can go lighter on non-science related classes like AP History or Computer Science.

During my freshman year, I heard how hard and time consuming AP World History would be. The massive shiny textbook was an intimidating 500+ pages long. Not being a natural history buff or having any interest in pursuing it, I decided to take regular World History. This was a critical choice that freed up my time to focus on extracurricular activities.

Next, do an "Extracurricular Time Audit"

When I saw my long list of extracurriculars, I realized that on paper I looked exactly the same as all the other honors kids. We were all in the same clubs: honor society, key club, academic decathlon, journalism, and so on.

I asked myself the same questions I did with my class audit. "Do I really enjoy these activities? Does it fit in with what I want to do in the future?"

Honestly, I didn't enjoy most of these activities. Like most of my classmates, I dutifully paid the honor society dues and spent time in these clubs because they were supposed to look good on college applications. I realized that college admissions officers would not be able to pick me out from the sea of identical applicants.

Thus, I decided to quit journalism, academic decathlon, and many other clubs to focus on my strengths.

It can be hard to quit

I know it's not easy to leave a club, especially when people are counting on you. I still remember the look on my journalism teacher's face when I told her I was leaving the journalism club. Her cherry red face turned into a frown of disappointment, disbelief, and resentment.

She said, "I don't know why you are doing this. We trained you to replace the seniors and become THE copy editor."

I responded, "While I appreciate my time in journalism and your training, I know it's not for me. I need to free up my time for debate."

It was painful to quit journalism, but as I left the classroom, I felt a huge wave of relief reinforcing that I was doing the right thing.

Quitting activities that don't interest you or relate to your career goal will free up enormous amounts of time. Coming up, you will learn how to use this "extra" time to explore your interests and create a project that actually helps you stand out.

ACHIEVE in action - Business example

Imagine that you are sure you want to become an entrepreneur. As a kid, you would see your parents buying and selling things on eBay, on Craigslist, and even trying to flip used cars. You know there are a lot of impressive applicants out there who are interested in business, so you need to find a way to stand out.

Step 1- Aim for As in Advanced Classes

You work on your ACHIEVE plan step-by-step to make sure that you are on the right track. First, you create a four-year plan for high school where you are taking all the AP classes that fit in your schedule and that are related to your business economics major. You also decide to take a small business class, Marketing 101, and a basic finance class at your local community college.

Step 2 - Conduct an Activity Audit

Then you move onto cutting activities. You have quite a few from when you were in 9th grade and tried to do everything. You decide to cut journalism, the community service club, and HOSA (after you realized how long medical school was, you decided that you didn't want to be pre-med).

Step 3 - Help your Teacher Help You

After that, you partner with your economics teacher, who happens to also be a small business owner whose family owns a small restaurant in the city center. You decide that it would be great to have a business club at school.

Step 4 - Ignite your Interests

After establishing your business club with your economics teacher as your club advisor, you reach out to your local chamber of commerce to get some speakers for your club. You also interview them to understand what their biggest issues are. You realize that one of the big issues is getting financing for the Spanish business owners.

Step 5 - Execute your Theme

You decide to work on a project to help tackle this issue. You partner with your Economics teacher, local banks, and the Chamber of Commerce to provide resources in Spanish.

Step 6 - Validate your credibility

Your local newspaper and TV channel love featuring people who help their community, and they hear about you from someone in the Chamber of Commerce. You save these news clippings for your application in senior year.

Step 7 - Earn your Target SAT / ACT score

Future Ivy

Since you don't have the financial resources for an ACT standardized test tutor, you enroll in a free Boot Camp online and take lots of practice tests for the ACT. You end up getting your target score of 34 out of 36.

You get admitted to UPenn, Cornell, and other great schools.

Summary

* In order to stand out, you need the time to do so.
* Doing an Activity Audit will free up the time for you to do the next steps in the ACHIEVE system. When you do this audit, cut out the activities and classes that don't relate to your future goals or that you don't enjoy anymore.
* Quitting can be hard, but being overwhelmed by a laundry list of activities is worse.
* Any time you feel overwhelmed and don't have enough time, do an activity audit.

Action Steps

- ☐ Conduct a "class time audit"
- ☐ Conduct an "extracurricular time audit"
- ☐ Cut your schedule down to 1-2 main activities ("do less but better")

CHAPTER 8

β

Step 3 of Achieve - Help your teacher help you

Senior year of high school I was voted Teacher's Pet and most likely to come back as a teacher. I loved teaching and tutoring others, so I thought the second label made sense, but the label of teacher's pet, not so much.

I wasn't the best student (I know because my teachers would say who got the highest test scores and essays, and I was never one of them). I actually felt that I was one of the worst students in terms of attendance among the top 10. I'm sure people thought I was best buddies with the teachers because I stayed to talk to them every break. In reality, I was always making up assignments and tests because I was always missing class for a debate tournament or internship.

Looking back, I realize that most students don't talk to their teachers, besides when called on in class. This is a problem when it comes to college admissions for a few reasons. The most obvious is that if you've never interacted with your teacher, then they won't have anything interesting to say about you and you'll look like the rest of the applicants.

The second reason is that you'll do better in the class if you get to know your teacher. This is because the more comfortable you are, the more likely you will ask for help when you need it. We've all had intimidating teachers who you wouldn't dare go to by yourself during break to ask a question.

The third reason is that teachers can serve as your mentor, providing you wisdom and practical advice along your career journey. For example, say you are interested in biology, so you go above and beyond in your biology class. You express interest to your teacher about doing research, and one day she tells you after class that she found a special opportunity for you.

She forwards you an email in which a biology professor from the local university is looking for a high school intern. She knows this professor personally, so upon your approval, she puts in a good recommendation and you get an interview. You ask your teacher if she can practice interviewing with you and she agrees to help you prepare. You end up rocking the interview and getting picked for this unique research opportunity. Your teachers can also help you write letters of support for prestigious and competitive summer programs and for full-ride scholarships.

Getting to know your teachers

When I was in 7th grade, I wanted to get better at Spanish, so I thought why not volunteer with my Spanish teacher to absorb more of the language.

He was a nice Polish guy with glasses and a beard who had a 7-syllable-long name that I remember to this day, since we practiced saying his name so much. During one break, I offered to help him organize papers and potentially grade assignments. His eyes lit up and he accepted my offer. So, every week I'd help grade homework assignments and tests and organize papers to prepare for the next class.

I thought the work was fun, as I was seeing what a teacher does outside the classroom and getting to know more about my Spanish teacher's journey.

In 8th grade, I did the same teacher's assistant volunteering role for my Geometry teacher. I learned things beyond Geometry, like how little teachers were paid, what tenure means (it's like a permanent job contract), and how teachers spend their time after a full day of teaching (hint - lots of paperwork).

These relationships helped me feel more comfortable approaching my teachers and made me realize that even the intimidating ones are in this job so they can help students. This meant I felt comfortable asking for clarification on confusing and simple concepts, so that it would never be too late to recover from a poor grade or exam failure.

How to become friends with your teachers

To develop a friendship with your teachers, find ways to be helpful, like volunteering when they need a guinea pig or participating in class (how would you feel if you were presenting and asked a question to the class and no one responded?). If you are nervous to participate, try to prepare some questions about the lecture material ahead of time and ask in class. Teachers notice those who participate!

You can also ask your teacher if they'd like to have you volunteer as a teacher's assistant. The key is to make it easy for them to say yes by listing out ways you can help them, such as putting together study guides, creating flashcards for the class, or helping to organize papers or digital files.

Once you start volunteering on a regular basis, use the time to get to know them better. For example, how did they become a teacher? What do they like to do for fun? You can also share more about yourself and your dreams, which ensures your teachers have the information to help you on your path.

For example, one of my coaching students is passionate about girl's education in Southeast Asia, e.g., Myanmar. She informed her 10th grade English teacher that she was attending a Harvard conference about the state of women there, and her teacher supported her missing class and was excited for her.

If, later on, this English teacher writes a letter of recommendation, it will show to the admissions officer that the student has been passionate about this topic for many years. (Side note: usually you want to ask for letters of recommendation from 11th grade teachers, but if you are still speaking to your 10th grade teacher on a regular basis, for instance if she has been advising your club for 3 years, that can be okay.) Dedication over time stands out, so get to know your teachers and keep them updated on your extracurriculars!

Skill: The Avocado Toast Method

How do you get to know your teachers and get them to be your mentors? How do you get to know your classmates and get them to date you? You give them value. If they love avocado toast, you make them avocado toast every day. If they are low in motivation because of the virtual learning environment, you give them genuine compliments about their teaching each class.

The Avocado toast method works like growing an avocado tree.[12] First, you'll need to find the right conditions, like when your teacher is in a good mood. Then, you'll plant the seed and start a conversation with your teacher. After that, you'll need to nurture the plant by watering it frequently and fertilizing once in a while. You can do this with your teacher by regularly participating in class and attending office hours. Much later, you will reap the rewards of avocados, AKA a wonderful friendship with your teacher who guides you on your career journey and writes you an outstanding letter of recommendation.

It works on the basic principle that you can earn someone's trust by making their day a little brighter every time you see them. It doesn't have to be avocado toast, it doesn't have to cost money, but it does have to be thoughtful and specific to that person. If we're talking about your teachers, it could be as simple as actively participating during every class.

It's not a get rich quick scheme, and you won't get someone to mentor you or even give you meaningful advice after the first time. There is no beginner's luck here. This method takes time, but it's worth it.

How can you make sure you are providing value? Ask the person. Ask them how you can help them and what their biggest challenge is. Then, brainstorm ways to make it easier for them. For example, your teacher might share that her biggest challenge is to get people to participate in class. You could decide to help research ways to increase participation and implement your ideas with your teacher's guidance.

The avocado toast method is about showing up every day and bringing small amounts of value to this person's life.

---

[12] https://www.wikihow.com/Grow-Avocados

ACHIEVE in action - Pre-med example

Let's imagine that you want to become a doctor. As a kid, you would accompany your father who had a myriad of health issues like diabetes, high blood pressure, and help translate for your immigrant dad. While this was scary and a lot of responsibility, you learned a lot being at the hospital and got to become friends with the doctors.

You know that the Ivy League gets a lot of applicants who are pre-med, so you need to find a way to stand out. You go through the steps of ACHIEVE to make sure that you are on the right track.

Step 1 - Aim for As in Advanced Classes

You find that you completed step one and are taking the most advanced classes, such as AP chem, AP bio, and even an anatomy class. You've also learned that you learn well with flashcards and by looking up complex concepts on YouTube. Once you are getting As in your classes, you take a look at the ACHIEVE system's next step.

Step 2 - Conduct an Activity Audit

The second step is to conduct an activity audit. When you list out all the activities that take up your time, you realize that you are a participant in honor society and academic decathlon but don't enjoy the activity anymore. You send an email to the club presidents that other priorities have come up and unfortunately you cannot continue.

Step 3 - Help your Teacher Help You

Now, with this free time, you use one of the lunches you would have spent attending those club meetings to meet with your biology teacher. You realize that one of the ways you can help her and the other students in the class is by finding fun YouTube videos that describe complex concepts. Your teachers and classmates all appreciate your work.

Step 4 - Ignite your Interests

Next, you work on igniting your interests so you can find your theme, and you reach out to your doctor for an informational interview. In the interview, you ask about opportunities for high school students to get involved, and she shares with you that she can't hire you since you're under 18 but that you can volunteer at the local teen health clinic. She forwards you an email that shows the local team clinic is looking for social media help.

Even though you're not a social media superstar, you learn the basics by watching YouTube videos. While you're volunteering at the teen health clinic, you realize that vaping is a huge concern. You brainstorm ways to spread awareness about the harmful effects of vaping and one of the ideas you've decided to execute is to create a social media campaign. For this campaign, you reach out to leading researchers and use your interviews with them to serve as the facts for a foundation to your posts.

Step 5 - Execute your Theme

You end up building a friendship with one of the researchers and she offers you a research assistant position.

Step 6 - Validate your credibility

Some of the research that you do leads to getting your name in a publication. Also, because of your hard work on the stop vaping social

Future Ivy

media campaign, your local newspaper emails you to feature your story. You save this news clipping for senior year college applications.

Step 7 - Earn your Target SAT / ACT score

At the end of junior year, you spend three months preparing for the ACT, and you earn your target score of 35 out of 36

You get admitted to Brown, Columbia, and other great schools.

Summary

- In step 3 of ACHIEVE, you learned that it's important to get to know your teachers so they can understand how to help you.
- Through the "Avocado Toast Method" of adding value, you develop a strong bond with your teachers. Because of that, you not only feel comfortable asking questions when you don't understand something but you also start participating in class and enjoying school more.
- Later, when you need a club advisor or a letter of recommendation, you know you can count on your teachers.

Action Steps

- ☐ Participate at least once in every class (it could be asking a question)
- ☐ Note down ways you can help make your teacher's life easier
- ☐ Go to 3 teacher's office hours or schedule a one-on-one (talk about your career choice)

Future Ivy

CHAPTER 9

β

Step 4 of ACHIEVE - Ignite your interests

When I was 14, a freshman, I walked into the high school career center, which was attached to the academic counseling offices. I started talking to Mrs. K, the tall, thin career counselor with a blonde bob haircut. She welcomed me to the career center and explained that it was a resource for all high school students.

I was very curious about this new place and asked her if she had any resources for figuring out what you would want to do in the future. She smiled and told me about aptitude tests—quizzes that give you a sense of what careers would be good for you based on your interests.

I asked to take one of these and promptly sat down at a nearby table to learn more about myself. After the short quiz, we discovered that practicing law could be a good fit. I was conflicted, because I had also wanted to be a doctor, but to my delight, Mrs. K advised me that I could combine the two. She told me that her brother was a pharmaceutical lawyer, which greatly piqued my interest.

I proclaimed, "Oh! I can do medical law."

Little did she know then that I would come into Harvard as a freshman telling everyone, "I want to be an international pharmaceutical lawyer." (International since I loved studying languages, too.) My college classmates still remember that, since I was so specific.

After seeing my excitement at combining my interests in medicine and law, Mrs. K recommended I talk to Mr. L, a history teacher who had previously been a lawyer. I thanked her and left her office feeling a sense of excitement to explore this new career path.

I still remember that day. Most of all, I remember that it was a rainy day and my mom had been patiently waiting after school for me. I thanked my mom for letting me stay late and for being supportive. Thank your parents! They do a lot to support you.

How to figure out what you want to do

1) Take an aptitude test.

They can help reveal what you are interested in. Take them with a grain of salt, though. Your career goals will evolve and change many times as you learn more about yourself.

If it recommends you a career as an architect and you have no interest in that, keep going down the list and find careers that interest you. These are crude tools, not some magical Harry Potter Sorting Hat. At the end of the day, you have to interpret the results yourself and decide what you want to explore.

Here are some resources that I recommend, but feel free to explore further:

- Minnesota State Career Cluster Interest Survey
- My Next Move Interest Profiler
- The MAPP™ Career Assessment Test

2) Write down a list of your interests.

Don't worry about the length of the list. Ask yourself, what classes have I enjoyed? What activities do I wake up on a Saturday morning and want to do? It's okay if it doesn't seem academic at first. What's important is that you are genuinely interested in it.

For example, maybe you enjoy watching videos on how to care for succulent plants and get super interested in the biology of plants, AKA botany. Or maybe you love coaching soccer on the weekends for junior high school students.

3) Find the intersections.

I was interested in medicine and law, so I combined them and explored medical law. What are things that you could combine on your list? Are you interested in neuroscience and swimming? Are you interested in drawing and history? Write down the potential intersections.

4) Pick one of the intersections to explore further.

Maybe it was neuroscience and swimming. So, you could look into the neuroscience of swimming. Or if you are interested in drawing and history, you can look into art history.

5) Spend at least 15 minutes every day feeding your interest.

Your interest is like a seed, and in order for it to grow, you need to give it energy and time. Gather books from your local library on these topics. Browse blogs and watch YouTube videos on your interests. Learn the common terms, trends, and where the field is headed.

Interview professionals in your field

Once you feel you have a firm grasp of a topic like botany, reach out to people in the field to see if you would like working with them and whether the culture in that job is aligned with your values.

For example, you might value innovation and a fast-paced environment, so you interview marketing managers at a local marketing firm who bring that up as part of their culture. Maybe you value having personal time to do hobbies like drawing, and when you interview journalists you discover that it would be difficult to maintain that hobby, since you work on tight deadlines.

I've done hundreds of interviews throughout my academic and professional career. It will help you learn what life is like for someone who actually does this job. Do they enjoy it? How did they get there? What are the day-to-day responsibilities?

In junior year of college, I was interested in luxury retail, so I reached out to as many people as I could who were in those roles at companies like Louis Vuitton, Chanel, and Burberry. Through those interviews, I learned how much these companies valued having experience in the stores (as they have the cash registers and drive sales), so I ended up applying to all the luxury stores in Boston and getting a job at Louis Vuitton. Because of my retail experience, I stood out when applying for internships and ended up at Bloomingdales for my junior summer of college. These interviews can help prepare you to break into the field and may lead to other opportunities.

Use your personal network

First, ask everyone that you know. I asked my career counselor about any lawyers she knew and she connected me with a teacher at my high school who was a lawyer. One of my students was interested in aerospace engineering and remembered that she had met an aerospace engineer at one of her family's social events.

One question to reflect on is this: who do I know that is well connected? Maybe it's a teacher who seems to know who's who in town, or maybe it's your best friend who is involved with a lot of volunteer programs.

For example, if you are interested in Chemistry and want to do research, ask your teachers, counselors, family, and friends if they know of any chemistry professors or opportunities to do research.

You will often come across, "I don't know anyone, but I'll keep you in mind." Please don't be discouraged! When someone says, "Actually, I do know someone," it can all be worth it.

This is about building relationships, and you simply have to keep trying. Always be respectful and grateful when asking for help. They may not be able to help you right away, but you can always ask them to keep you in mind when they come across something.

Once you exhaust asking everyone you know, you'll need to reach out to people you don't know. In sales, these are called "cold leads," whereas people you have a personal introduction to are called "warm leads." Although you are more likely to land an interview with a warm lead, there are many more cold leads out there, so the opportunities are limitless.

How to get an interview with people you don't know

Skill: Online Outreach

"Online Outreach" is when you email someone you don't know but want to know. This is also known as "cold emailing" or "networking." And just like you wouldn't text someone you barely know with a huge list of requests, you're not going to bombard people with tons of questions. It's really just one question: "I'm really interested in your career, could you tell me a bit more about how you got started?"

People love to talk about themselves, so give them the opportunity. You can use this approach with getting to know your teachers as well. Start with curiosity and respect, simply by asking questions!

The Online Outreach email is especially useful when reaching out to professionals, professors, alumni, the president, etc. Really, anyone. There's nothing stopping you from cold emailing a University president and somehow being able to talk to him. I suggest you be more targeted and perhaps email a specific professor in the department that you are interested in, but you get my point. You can reach out to anyone with cold emailing, and the best thing is, the worst that can happen is that you don't hear back. You get ignored. Most likely lost in the piles of emails of busy people, but ignored nonetheless. Yes, it can definitely feel horrible to be ignored after you've put so much mental effort into your emails, but at the end of the day, it's not that bad.

Even if you never hear from them, things will be okay, plus there's tons of other people out there. It really is a numbers game, and the person who sends out the most messages is going to get the most replies and opportunities and therefore feel less doubt. And of course, I have some techniques to always get a reply. I've learned that persistence and a positive attitude toward meeting new people is the key.

In order to simplify online outreach emailing, I want to focus on the single best way to use this technique. It also happens to be the best way to meet people, get informal internships, get jobs, land interviews, and overall build great relationships. Cold emailing to get informational interviews. You can get anywhere with informational interviews. My student Cali tried this out and in one summer got three different remote internship opportunities in mechanical engineering. No joke, she was working on rocket parts by the end of the summer, all because she took a chance and cold emailed dozens of companies and research sites that she found online.

You can reach out to mentors online, such as people you find have an interesting job. You can also meet mentors at school, clubs, and teams that you're a part of. The more varied, the better. I would rather have different mentors from different fields advising me little by little than only one mentor to deal with all my issues.

You'll learn this about college, but most students I talk to told me that being exposed to different ways of thinking and different perspectives from students from all over the world was one of the most life-changing aspects of going to college. Different perspectives from different mentors will also help you figure out your next career step..

Finding Mentors

Thinking back, entering the career office that day not only made me realize my interest in medical law, but more importantly, it started something even more valuable—a friendship with a new mentor. This is really important: mentors will accelerate your success. Mentors can introduce you to new opportunities and other mentors. This is what happened to me. Mrs. K told me to reach out to Mr. L, a history teacher at school who had been a lawyer, so I did.

I found his classroom with some difficulty, and upon entering the classroom, I spotted a rotund gentleman with a shiny bald head wearing a brown coat who was deep in conversation with the much shorter but elegant AP English teacher.

I sheepishly approached them and respectfully interrupted their conversation to introduce myself, telling him that Mrs. K, the career counselor, had recommended I talk to him because I was interested in becoming a medical lawyer. He graciously replied, "I no longer practice law, but luckily I do have a friend who practices medical law just 20 minutes from here. I can reach out to him if you'd like?" I quickly responded, "That would be amazing!"

Mr. L did reach out to his friend and even set up a meeting for my mom and I. A week later, we met with his friend at his law office and created an unpaid informal internship wherein I would shadow him, file legal documents, and do research once a week.

Maybe you are interested in architecture and you don't know anyone who knows someone in this field.

There are three strategies for reaching out to professionals. First, you can use social media networks like LinkedIn to connect with professionals in your field of interest and send them a personalized message saying you are interested in their career path.

You can send a short message when you request to connect so that you don't have to pay to send them a LinkedIn message. On their profile, click "Connect" and "add a note."

Here's a template you can use for LinkedIn. You need to keep it short due to the character restrictions:

Hi [Name],

I'm currently a [grade e.g. sophomore] at [your high school] and interested in [industry, e.g. marketing]. I'm curious if you enjoy working in [industry] and if you'd recommend it? Would really appreciate a quick 15-20 min call or coffee to learn more!

Thanks,

[Your Name]

Second, you can find their emails online (a lot of professors have emails online) and send them a short email.

Here's a template you can use for an email:

Hi [Name],

I'm currently a [grade e.g, sophomore] at [your high school] and interested in [industry e.g., marketing]. I saw your amazing research in [research paper topic e.g., MEMS and sensors materials] and wanted to reach out.

I'm curious about your career path in [industry, e.g., engineering] and [something notable in their career, e.g., "your change in profession from management consultant to an Engineering professor"].

I was wondering if you would be open to a quick 15-20 min call or coffee to learn more about your perspectives on the industry and if you'd recommend pursuing [industry, e.g., engineering]!

Thanks,

[Your Name]

Quantity can help

Do this for at least 10 people. Many people won't respond, but a few will. Those few are your doors to opportunities. Thank them profusely and take as many notes as you can during the call or meeting.

* Before your call, make sure to have a list of questions that are specific to them and the industry they are in.
* Note that an informational interview is NOT the right time to ask for a job or internship. You need to build rapport with this person and ideally provide some value to them. This is

your opportunity to impress them with your insider knowledge and initiative. You will ask about job shadowing opportunities and internships in your follow up "Thank you" note.

Here are some great questions you can use:

- I noticed that X is happening in the job industry. What are your thoughts on it?
- Why did you choose this career?
- How did you get into this job?
- How would you describe the perfect person for this job?
- What's the most important preparation for a role like yours? What can I do in high school?
- What do you wish someone would have told you before you started this career?
- How do you think this job will change over the next 10 years?
- What's it like to work at your company? What's the day-to-day like?
- What's the biggest challenge in your job?
- What's the biggest pro and con of your job?

Toward the end of the call (if the chemistry feels right), you should thank them and ask if they know of any opportunities or colleagues that would be willing to talk to you. Remember that one professional can introduce you to many others in your field of interest.

After the call, you should follow up within 1-2 days with a thank you message and include that you'd love an opportunity to job shadow or do an internship.

Here's an example "Thank You Note":

Dear [Name],

Thank you so much for taking the time to speak with me about the [job title] role [today/yesterday]. I really enjoyed our conversation and [hearing about/learning about] [something that you discussed]. Also, I loved learning about [something that you discussed].

I am very excited about this career and feel that my interests in [share relevant aspects of your background] would make me a great fit for being a [job title].

I'd love an opportunity to job shadow or do an internship if available.

Thank you again,

[Your Name]

If you do this with enough professionals, you will likely land an opportunity to shadow, intern, or simply gain a valuable mentor that will keep you in mind for unique opportunities.

The third way to get interviews is to join interest groups and organizations. Say you are interested in animal sciences. Is there a local museum for animal sciences or a professional group for vets? Reach out to them and see if you can join a meeting.

After conducting your interview, you'll be more sure in your career direction, which will help you pick the best extracurriculars for your application and ones that you'll enjoy.

If you eventually discover that you are not interested in this topic anymore, you're still making progress. The point is to learn more about yourself. I did a chemistry internship at my local university and realized

Future Ivy

that I didn't enjoy lab work, which would have been a good chunk of my time if I decided to go into pre-med.

Maybe you discover that your interest is your passion! Bingo! You are one step closer to standing out to the Ivy League. Your passion will be the source of your passion portfolio, which I'll explain in the next chapter.

ACHIEVE in action - Art example

Imagine that you are extremely into Art. Your parents love photography and your older sister is a graphic designer. You love helping them out brainstorming new ideas and are sure that you want to have an artistic career.

You know the creative space is crowded and it can be difficult to stand out, so you use the ACHIEVE system to make sure you have the right strategy.

Step 1 - Aim for As in Advanced Classes

First you realize that your math grade needs a facelift. You go to your teacher's office hours and brainstorm ways that you can understand the math concepts better. One of the things you come up with is to review all the wrong answers from your homework assignments and exams every week. This ends up helping you feel good about math.

Step 2 - Conduct an Activity Audit

When you do your activity audit, you realize you're in some clubs that no longer excite you. For example, you enjoyed this mentorship program, but you don't enjoy it anymore in the virtual environment. You also used to think that maybe you wanted to be a doctor, so you joined the health science club, but now you know that you don't want that career. You quit these two clubs so you have more time to work on things that will help you stand out.

Step 3 - Help your Teacher Help You

One of the ideas that you had was to create an art therapy club. You bring this up with your teacher and she is quite excited about this, so you work with your guidance counselor to submit the necessary requirements to get the club started. You brainstorm different clubs that you could partner with, like the senior citizens health club, and develop different ways to help them, such as sponsoring an art therapy session for seniors.

To get the word out about this new club, you create a social media platform and make helpful posts about how you can use art in your life as therapy. For example, creative writing prompts, easy quick drawings, relaxation coloring books, and more. You quickly gain some popularity in your school and community, which helps you recruit club officers to help you get this off the ground.

Step 4 - Ignite your Interests

Once the club is started and you've got a few events under your belt, you start contacting freelance graphic designers and local photographers to learn more about the industry and how you can break in. At these interviews, you learn that one of the biggest challenges to break into the industry is to have a personalized and strong portfolio of your work. However, most young artists don't have anyone to get feedback from on their portfolio, and so they end up getting rejected for a lot of jobs.

Step 5 - Execute your Theme

You brainstorm some potential solutions and follow up with the people you interviewed to see if they are interested in helping out. The one idea that stuck out the most was to set up a once-a-month portfolio review where artists can submit their work to get a free review from experts. Because you did your research and this is a huge problem for artists, this program is successful and ends up getting sponsored by your local art museum.

Step 6 - Validate your Credibility

To add to your credibility, you ask your mentor to submit a letter of recommendation speaking about your art therapy club leadership and your initiative with the portfolio review program.

Step 7 - Earn your Target SAT / ACT score

For the standardized test, you decide that you're going to take the SAT three times to get your target score and spend the next three months drilling problems daily. You end up getting your target score of 1560 on the last try.

You end up getting into Yale, NYU, and other great schools.

Summary

* In step 4 of ACHIEVE, you gained some tools to figure out what you really want to do in life.
* You can take aptitude tests, write down all your interests, and find the intersections. Spending even 15 minutes per day exploring your intersections can help clarify your goals.
* You also learned that online research is not enough to pick a career, and you will have to talk to real professionals in your desired field. In order to do this, you learned the skill of "Online Outreach," which is basically cold-emailing professionals you don't know to set up an informational call.
* You can refer back to this chapter for the templates to reach out.

Action Steps

- ☐ Take an aptitude test online
- ☐ Reflect on careers that combine your interests
- ☐ Reach out to 10 professionals in the fields that you are interested in online or through family/friends/counselors

Future Ivy

CHAPTER 10

β

Step 5 of ACHIEVE

By now, you've researched your interests, some of the careers available to you, professionals in the field, and have even talked to some of them through Zoom. Hopefully by now you've also noticed a "theme" to your interests, because it's time to write it down.

Your application theme

Your why is your underlying motivation for wanting to go to a top university. Your theme is the path that you choose to get there. Think about climbing a mountain. The top is that Ivy League diploma that's going to unlock jobs and opportunities for you. Your theme is the specific path that you go by. Some are steep and fast, some are windy and long. Either way, you need specific tools for each. If your theme is windy and long, you want to prepare with extra resources and comfy shoes. In a way, you have to prove to others that you are ready to endure the long road.

The number one biggest mistake that I see students make is not having an application theme. What is an application theme? If you have a long list of extracurriculars that are random, then you don't have an application theme.

An applicant with a theme would curate activities and classes related to their interests. For example, I was interested in medical law, so I picked classes that would prepare me for all the reading and writing in law school, e.g., AP English, and I took community college English classes. For activities, I participated on the community college debate team, got a law internship, and got involved with my local city government. When an admissions officer reviews my application, it is clear what I'm passionate about and what my career direction will be.

You may also have heard of the theme being referred to as a spike or niche. These all echo the idea that building a story around who you are and what you care about will help you stand out from the crowd of students who have no clue what they want to do.

To stand out, think like an artist

If you are an artist applying for a creative role, would you bring them only one sample of your work? No! You'd bring a portfolio of your work so they can see the style of art that you can do and what you focus on.

Just like an artist, start to think about your college application as a portfolio of activities and classes. One thing you may have come across is the passion project, which is where you start your own extracurricular, such as a mental health awareness social media brand. It's important to note that one passion project is not enough. Many students can start a debate club or a blog, so how do you stand out?

Passion portfolios are the secret

While doing one independent project, like starting a mentorship group for girls interested in STEM, may not be enough, you can combine different projects over time to demonstrate your theme. MIT Dean of Admission Stu Schmill said, "The portfolios that students can submit showing the independent work they've done can really enhance their applications."[13]

There are a few types of passion portfolio builders, so pick 2-3 that you want to pursue in your high school career.

7 Passion portfolio builders

1) Internships

Internships are a way to "try" a job before committing to a career. They could be short and take only a month, or go for years if you enjoy them and your boss sees your value. For example, you might want to be a lawyer, but after interning with a lawyer you realize that they don't get as much time in court as you wanted. You also learn that you dislike working in an office all day. This new information helps you move closer to a better career for you.

Not only are internships a great way to show proof of your career direction, they are a great way to expand your personal network, which can accelerate your ability to make an impact. For example, you may want an internship with a general medicine doctor and you might also want to help the community through educating the public on vaccination clinic locations. You tell your boss about this, and she helps connect you to her friend who works at a local medical marketing company. That friend helps you get traction on social media and increase your reach.

While you may be able to find an internship by applying online, there are honestly not that many internships for high school students. That's why they can help you stand out. You can create your own

---

[13] https://www.youtube.com/watch?v=-u3xaicPnA0

internships by meeting people in your field through informational interviews. That's how I landed my legal internship when I was 14.

2) Research assistant

These are roles where you get to work with a professor at a university to further knowledge in their field. They are great for showing your potential as a STEM (science, technology, engineering, math), pre-med, or future graduate school student.

This is a way to "test" if you'd like a career path in research. I did a chemistry internship at a local university and realized the lab environment wasn't for me. If I didn't test this, who knows if I would be in med school right now dreading each day. The more you try out different career paths and experiences, the more likely you will find a career that makes you happy.

To find research assistant positions, I would start by looking at the local universities near you. They may offer a summer internship opportunity for high school students, as my local university did. Even if they don't, you can create your own opportunity by cold emailing the professors for an informational interview. In the informational interview, you would find out what you can do to help them. The more you help people, the more they will help you.

3) Your own organization

Starting your own organization is a great way to stand out. Depending on what you found to be your theme, this could be a variety of things, including starting a debate club, a mental health awareness organization, or a small business.

This can help you stand out because it shows proof of what you're interested in, your leadership skills, and lets you find ways to give back to your community. You also don't have to wait for anyone, as you can start your organization today. You are the boss!

To get started, do some reflection around why your organization exists, what problems it helps address, and when you can work on it. For example, you might realize how few women become software engineers, so you develop conferences and mentorship circles to support more women in software engineering. You decide to spend your free period every Monday, Tuesday, and Friday working on this project to make a difference.

4) Professional organization

There are already a lot of established organizations out there that you could become a leader in. For example, if you're interested in health careers, there's an organization called HOSA. For business, there is DECA. Many of these organizations have leadership boards at the state and national level.

While top students may be the president of their local club chapter, you could stand out by aiming for the national or international positions. For example, one of my students was able to get a national level position at the PTSA organization, and that helped her stand out and get into Harvard.

To get started, I would research what professional organizations exist in your field of interest. Then look at their websites and see how the elections work for national and even international positions. If you don't apply, what are your chances of getting that position? Zero. But if you do apply, they're greater than zero.

5) Competitions

Many of you have asked whether you need awards to get into the Ivy League. Well, while not absolutely necessary, the competitions do help admissions officers understand where you rank in the world for your theme. For example, there are many students that apply to be math majors. Suppose Sally is a great math student and so is Bob, i.e., they have equal levels of talent in math; however, Sally decides to enter a national competition and wins. While Sally and Bob might have the same intellectual potential, Sally has more proof of her theme.

The best competitions to enter in order to stand out are ones that have national and international levels. Notable names and companies can also help you stand out, like Google or Intel's competition.

To get started, look up the biggest and most prestigious competitions in your intended major and area of interest. Then, look up the eligibility and application requirements and try out. If you don't try, you have a 100% chance of losing. Plus, you might learn something about the fields or meet new people in the competitions.

6) Selective summer programs

There are many summer programs out there and many of them do not help you stand out. The way you determine whether a program is good for your passion portfolio is by seeing whether the application process is extremely selective, as in below 20%. Also, if the program offers full scholarships and does not cost a lot of money, this also indicates that it's a competitive program.

Summer programs are a great way to explore your career interests and meet other students and professors in this field. This can help you in getting research assistant positions or in meeting people who are equally as motivated as you. It can spark your idea for an organization that you want to start and add to your passion portfolio.

Research science institute (RSI) is a great summer program that is free and gives you the opportunity to work with scientists at MIT.

7) Sports

Sports are a great way to stand out, especially if you can rank highly at the state and national level for your sport. Whether you play soccer or you run cross country, your dream school's athletic department may be looking for you. If you do wish to continue your sport in college, make sure to research whether the schools on your college list offer the sport at a varsity level.

As a student athlete, it's good to be familiar with the National Collegiate Athletic Association (NCAA) rules, as they are the nonprofit that regulates the student athlete world.

To get started,[14] make sure to register with the NCAA for eligibility and look up your dream schools' instructions to contact the coaches.[15] For example, on Harvard's athletic website, it says "to contact the respective head coach, who will send a recruiting questionnaire or direct you to Harvard's online recruiting forms."

There are certain NCAA rules for when they can chat with you. For example, in some sports, the coaches can't reach out until after your junior year.[16] When I interviewed a Harvard recruited athlete, he revealed that demonstrated interest is important as an athlete, meaning that you should be genuinely interested in the school. Since coaches can only recommend a handful of athletes to admissions, they are going to prefer the ones most likely to attend if accepted. I mean, how would you feel if

---

[14] https://web3.ncaa.org/ecwr3/

[15] https://gocrimson.com/sports/2020/5/5/information-recruiting-helpfulinfo.aspx

[16] https://gocrimson.com/sports/2020/5/5/information-recruiting-recruiting-rules.aspx

you stuck out your neck for a student and then they ended up picking another school?

Brainstorm your passion portfolio builders

Now it's time to brainstorm possible projects that can help you decide if the career you've chosen is the one for you. Your passion project should be something that combines your unique interests, i.e., pharmaceutical law, and helps you connect with people in that industry or even try it out for yourself. Yes, YouTube is amazing, but you won't know what working at a law office, or anywhere else, is like until you try it yourself.

I recommend starting your project as a "Reporter." Your job is to learn everything you can about this industry, and that will involve online research as well as talking to real people in the field. You can think about making an impact by helping other students learn about this topic and understand what a career in the field can look like. Think about a blog, YouTube channel, or podcast that shares helpful information with other students. These types of projects can be tied to raising money for a specific cause or geared to helping yourself and your friends get internships.

The key point is that being a "reporter" means that you are not an "expert." You are learning along with your audience and asking real "experts" how they got there. This is an easy way to approach your project and know that with consistent research, if you're truly passionate about this topic, you will stop feeling like an outsider.

Learning what you like and don't like is the most important part of this step. That's why it's great to try lots of things and see what resonates. You always win if you can learn from an experience, good or bad. When you find that you aren't interested in a certain intersection, go back to the other intersections you wrote down and choose another one to explore.

If it's not clear yet, this next step is going to help you brainstorm potential passion projects that will help you stand out.

Some questions to inform your brainstorm include:

- What projects relate to your future career goal or can help you develop the skills for your career goal?
- What projects help your community or school?
- What projects excite you so much that you'd rather work on them than watch Netflix on a Friday night?
- What projects sound impressive? Will it make people say, "Wow, how did you do that?"
- What projects push you outside your comfort zone?

Pick the project to start

Once you have a list of ideas, narrow them down to the best idea by asking yourself these questions. Ideally, you would answer yes to all or most of the following.

Does this project relate to your future career goal or help you develop the skills for your career goal? Colleges want to see that you have a direction towards a career, as this shows that you have been learning about yourself and your maturity.

Does this project help your community or school? An admissions officer is not just looking for students who can do well academically. They are also looking for students who will give back to the college community, participate in seminar classes, work well with others, and be great toward their roommates. College is as much a social affair as it is intellectual.

Does this project excite you, and would you pick it over watching Netflix on a Friday night? You want to pick a project that excites you so that you have the motivation to work on it. This will likely be after your hours of honors and AP homework and on the weekdays Thus, make sure your project passes the Friday Night Netflix Test.

Does the project sound impressive? Cal Newport in his book *How to Be a High School Superstar* explains that "accomplishments that are hard to explain are better than accomplishments that are hard to do." For example, becoming a best-selling author is harder to explain than starting a high school band (which is a lot of hard work too!). A good test for this is will it make people say, "Wow, how did you do that?"

Impressive projects are easy to explain in one sentence, like with a good slogan. To do this, you should think about what would be the outcome of your project. For example, my Harvard classmate invented a "one-minute mobile charger." Another example is writing a best-selling book in your field. The more sloganable your project, the more "wow" factor it will have.

Does this project push you outside your comfort zone and thus make you feel a little or a lot uncomfortable? Top schools want to see that you are pushing your academic and personal potential, which means getting outside your comfort zone and doing well in challenging classes. When you challenge yourself, you foster creativity, learn what activities you enjoy, and discover all the amazing things you are capable of.

You can also ask your teachers, counselor, or other mentors to help you with picking one to start. Ultimately, you need to pick the project that excited you the most and fits in with your career goals the best.

For example, I pursued law/medical internships and jobs that cultivated my career interest in medical law. I also joined my local community college's debate team and competed in college-level debate tournaments in order to develop public speaking skills (essential for lawyers). Later, I would start my high school's debate team and help other students conquer their fears of public speaking. The key is to curate activities that align with your theme in your passion portfolio.

Skill: Finding your theme

Your theme is your passion, skills, and problems all together.

(Passions + Skills + Problems) = Theme

One of my students is passionate about STEM, skilled in networking, and hates how few women are in STEM. After following the theme formula, she discovered her theme and created mentoring groups for more girls to break into STEM fields.

To figure out your application theme, reflect on the questions below and find a way you can combine your passion, skills, and a cause you care about into a theme.

To find your passions, ask yourself: What subjects do you know a lot about or enjoy talking about (e.g., anime, climate change, cooking)? What careers/fields interest you?

To find your skills: What skills do you know from previous classes, clubs, or academic programs? What topics do other people come to you for advice for?

To find your problem to solve, reflect on these questions: If you had a magic wand, what problem would you want solved? What problems break your heart?

One of my students is passionate about robotics and AI and skilled at coding. His theme is around educating the next generation how to use technology in a productive way and introduce them to careers in technology.

My theme in high school was about equipping high school students with knowledge of current events and learning communication skills through the debate team I founded.

Whatever your theme you pick, it will then be much easier to pick a project with which to start!

ACHIEVE in action - Law example

Imagine that you want to become a lawyer. Ever since your aunt became a lawyer and told you about the profession, you've been fascinated by it. Between watching Law & Order, practicing mock trials, and reading up on the latest Supreme Court cases, you can't get enough of it.

You know, though, that there's a lot of people who want to be lawyers and who apply to top schools like Harvard, so you make sure that you are on the right track to standing out with the ACHIEVE system.

Step 1 - Aim for As in Advanced Classes

When you take a look at the different steps in order, you realize that you're doing great and taking advanced classes and getting As.

Step 2 - Conduct an Activity Audit

You don't have many activities to cut. In fact, you're already really good at only doing the things you enjoy and that contribute to your future career goals.

Step 3 - Help your Teacher Help You

When you look at step three, you realize that you could develop a better relationship with your teachers. You are especially fond of your history teacher, so you decide to start going to office hours to get to know him better. You realize that there is a great need for more visual content that is engaging in the history class, and your history teacher would love to have more skits and videos as part of the teaching material.

You put together a proposal to recruit people in the drama program to act out some of the most important things to remember from history. You also decide to recruit the film department, who mainly films athletic activities but who might be up for this. Your teacher is ecstatic and helps you contact the head of the drama department and also the film department so you can get started.

After developing a great relationship with your history teacher and kicking off this project, you decide to move onto the next step.

Step 4 - Ignite your Interests

You know that you want to be a lawyer, so you reach out to lawyers and judges in your community for informational interviews.

Through your interviews, you learn about an opportunity to volunteer at youth court. Because you attend this court every week and make an effort to go above and beyond by helping set up and staying afterwards to put things away, you develop a great relationship with the program director and the judge. You express your interest in a legal internship to a judge, and since he has many connections in the space, he connects you to one of his past classmates from law school.

Step 5 - Execute your Theme

Future Ivy

This lawyer is looking for help organizing and filing his documents, and you are up for the challenge. Slowly, you begin to take on more responsibility. For example, you start helping take notes during some of the expert interviews. She also brings you along to the court cases so you can see things like how the jury gets selected.

Step 6 - Validate your Credibility

After feeling like your internship is in a good spot, you start to beef up your credibility by submitting articles about your experience to local publications. While it takes a few months to get a feel for what types of articles the publications like, you eventually get one article into a big-name publication in the law space. You ask your law mentor to submit a letter of recommendation and she gladly accepts. You've helped her so much with organization and optimism, so she wants to help you as well.

Step 7- Earn your Target SAT / ACT score

You are a natural test-taker, so the SAT is no problem for you and end up getting your target score and applying to 12 colleges.

You end up getting admitted to Harvard and Dartmouth!

Summary

- In step 5 of ACHIEVE, you learned the difference between your "why" and your "theme."
- You also learned about the 7 types of Passion Portfolio builders, which can help you discover your unique way of standing out.
- Then you learned how to find your theme by combining your passion, skills, and a cause you care about.
- Finally, you can reflect on a series of questions that will help you brainstorm what type of project you should do and how to make sure that it is impactful, challenging, and related to your future goals.

Action Steps

- ☐ Define your application theme
- ☐ Identify which types of projects you want in your passion portfolio
- ☐ Narrow down to one project to start

Future Ivy

CHAPTER 11

β

Step 6 of ACHIEVE - Validate your credibility

"Youth making a difference." "Driven to medicine—and law." These were the two headlines for the two articles written about me in local newspapers. When I was applying to colleges, I made sure to include them to show that I was a leader in my community. This helped me stand out among other students in my region and secure a spot in the Ivy League.

When you are applying to the Ivy League, you are competing against top students with awesome extracurriculars. How are you supposed to stand out with your passion portfolio vs. someone else? That's why it's important to validate your credibility, AKA to show proof that you are a thought leader in your theme. There are many ways to validate your credibility including getting published, winning awards, building a significant following, partnering with well-known brands, getting a thought leader in your space to write a recommendation letter, or showing your impact.

One of the Ivy League students I interviewed who had read his admission file revealed that by submitting his piano recording, he had validated his talent over and above the numerous piano awards he had won. This helped the admission committee be confident in his skills and admit him. Anyone could say they are a world-class pianist, but without the proof, very few will believe it.

Increasing your impact

Future Ivy

Having an impact in your community shows proof that you will likely contribute to the college community. For example, maybe you help spread awareness about the vaccine clinics and get 100 people to sign up. Starting a project is great, but making a difference is better.

Once you have your project going, think about how you can increase its impact. Could you partner with clubs at other schools? Can you blog about what you learned and teach others how to do something similar?

Increasing your project's impact can take many forms depending on your goals. If you are on a science track, you might not be published in Science magazine, but you can certainly get a mentor's attention by showing your interest in a specific career and possibly land some internships. Yes, getting an internship, especially with well-known companies, can increase your credibility and thus your project's impact. Being able to raise more money or get more people involved are other ways to increase your impact.

Admissions officers are looking for evidence that you are doing your best to help your community, and don't get me wrong, you can do a lot of good by yourself. Maybe you are going door to door, or zoom to zoom, selling candy bars to raise money for your local church.

Now, imagine if you get some of your friends involved, or start posting on social media and schools across the country love your ideas so much that they want to help you out. Using social media can help open up tons of opportunities, including the chance to build up your team so that your ideas have a much bigger impact. It can give you the chance to assume a leadership role and coordinate a nationwide fundraiser that reaches thousands of kids. It may seem a little out there at first, but usually the hardest part is starting the project, and increasing its impact will be easier and come with time.

There are many ways you can increase your impact. If you are doing research at a local college, could you present the material at a conference? Submit your work to get published? Maybe you can teach other students how to get a research position?

Using Social Media

Social media can be a great tool in building an audience that can help you increase the awareness of your problem. Say you started a debate team and you wanted to expand your impact by improving communications skills outside of your school. You can use social media to reach people all around the world and teach public speaking skills. Whether you use YouTube, Instagram, TikTok, Twitter, or Medium, you can share your experience and expertise, which will serve as evidence of your impact in your community and beyond.

If you do choose to use social media, and you build up a big enough audience, it can be easier to contact influencers in your field. Many influencers are looking to expand their reach, and you can provide value by sharing their book, their research, their "whatever" to your audience.

Media attention

When you apply to colleges, attach any media attention you get. Whether it's an article about you in a local newspaper or a large, well-known blog, published articles/features show colleges your ingenuity and dedication. Sometimes newspapers will come to you and ask to write about you. When I was in high school, I had two local newspapers feature me for the work I was doing in the community, including putting on a teen job training seminar.

Some newspapers do a community profile of a person or have a section to feature teens. Find out what sections you might be a good fit for and get in touch with that section's editor. Journalists are always looking for the great next story!

If they don't come to you, you can pursue them. Build relationships with the journalists in your area or in your field and try to get to know them. Start by reading their work and sending them encouraging comments and questions. Then you can send them a pitch to be featured in their section.

PR Pitches

You can then pitch them an idea of something their readers would like. Do some research and make sure your work is related to the writer's target area. For example, Darrell Etherington is TechCrunch's Science Editor; he uses Twitter to request pitches.

An example pitch:

Hi [Name],

I've been following your work for the last year and love your insights on [industry].

Your recent post on [Topic] really resonated with me and reminded me of the project I'm currently working on: [impact and benefits of your project].

You can read more about it here: [insert link with blog of more info].

If this interests you, I'd love to share it with your audience.

Thank you again for your insights and tips in the [industry, e.g., mechanical engineering] industry.

Best Wishes,

[Your Name]

Remember that you will likely have to pitch many journalists multiple times to get a story published. However, if you are consistent and continue to grow these relationships, you not only may get a published article or feature with your name on it but also a valuable new mentor. If you do get published, make sure to save the article so you can include it with your college application.

An important part of pitching yourself is being able to communicate what you can actually bring to the table, your value. A great way to practice this is to write your resume. You can include your school activities in your resume in place of working experience.

Skill: resume writing for impact

"The tallest blade of grass gets cut down," my mom would repeatedly tell me as a way to keep me humble. It seems like a profound Chinese proverb, but in reality, at least in today's fast charging and moving world, it is an outdated philosophy.

In my first job after college, I remember coming to my first annual performance review with a list of my accomplishments. My boss was astounded by how much I did, even though he met with me on a weekly basis and knew the projects I was working on. I learned that if you don't share your wins and your value, it's likely that no one will notice it. This applies in your college application too. If you are too humble about your accomplishments, your admissions officer might not recognize your great value to the school.

For example, say you were a translator for your school's soccer team that competed internationally. In your resume or activities section of the application, you might simply write that you "translated for the soccer team during tournaments." It's true, of course, but would a reader understand how you helped the team succeed?

An admissions officer might look at this and not find it very impressive, because you have not been very specific about your impact.

This is a real story of an applicant who translated for Olympic level teams but never even mentioned it on their application. If you've ever traveled somewhere where you didn't know the language, I'm sure you can appreciate how important it is to have a guide to help you avoid mistakes and navigate through the country. While this student helped his team stay healthy and find everything they needed at the highest levels of the game, not bragging about it almost cost him admission. Luckily, one of his letters of recommendation mentioned his international impact and high level of professionalism with translations.

I've learned the following tips on how to artfully brag after investing thousands in career coaching and can't wait to share them with you. To write your resume bullets and show your impact use this formula: result + action.

For example, say you partnered with local schools to do an auction. Great, now how can we spice up this description? Start with the result. Mention how many schools participated. Numbers and specific details help the reader understand how impressive this effort was.

"Raised 13,550 dollars for Habitat for Humanity by coordinating an auction with three schools." You can keep adding details, but talk about the impact right away and then the specific actions that you took.

To find the result or impact, ask yourself, "So what?" In the last example, you partnered with three high schools to organize an auction fundraiser.

"Cool, but so what?" And you might answer, "Well, this helped raise 10,000 dollars for Habitat for Humanity." BINGO! That's the result!

Here are some more examples:

- Raised 10,000 dollars for Habitat for humanity by partnering with three high schools to organize an auction fundraiser.
- Helped 27 students prioritize mental wellbeing through organization of 5 mental wellness workshops and 45+ motivational posts on social media
- Connected 17 high school females to leading tech experts by creating a mentorship program to inspire more females to go into STEM

ACHIEVE in action - Math example

Let's imagine you love math. Ever since you got to compete with your little sister on multiplication, you loved being able to get the right answer and get it the fastest.

Step 1 - Aim for As in Advanced Classes

In school, you place into the most advanced math track so that you would be taking AP Calculus B/C in senior year. You even decide to take a theoretical algebra class during your junior year to stretch yourself. Even though you feel confident in math, you feel lost regarding how to stand out. You know that the Ivies get lots of kids who score perfect scores on the math section of the SAT.

You start from step 1 of the ACHIEVE system and focus on getting your B in AP English up to an A. You start reviewing drafts of your essays with your teacher to make sure you are on the right track.

Step 2 - Conduct an Activity Audit

Then you move to step 2. You realize you are in a bunch of clubs that you joined because of your friends who now aren't even in them. You decide to quit chess club, photography club, and a community service club.

Step 3 - Help your Teacher Help You

Now with your extra two hours a week, you decide to help your math teacher. You survey your friends about their biggest challenges with learning math and the one thing you discover is that a lot of students aren't motivated to learn it because they don't understand how it applies in the real world. They wish it was less theoretical and more practical. You work with your teacher to bring in real world examples like how the P value is used in marketing to determine which advertisement does better.

Step 4 - Ignite your Interests

After building a friendship with your teacher and regularly contributing to class, you move onto the next step - igniting your theme search. You research careers that would be good for math lovers and stumble upon data science. You do some research on the job market and find promising trends. You find an online conference for data science that you register for. The conference happens during school, so you email your teachers to get their permission. They all say yes and your math teacher is excited for you!

You learn so much from the conference, even though you didn't understand some of the words they used. You email one of the speakers that you have the most in common with and ask for a short phone call. She doesn't respond so you follow up with another email. The next day, you are surprised to see that she responded with some times she's available.

You chat with her and ask her some extremely well-researched questions. She's impressed! You follow up after the call with a nice thank you note and ask for an opportunity to job shadow. She's happy to help you and this job shadowing opportunity turns into an internship.

Step 5 - Execute your Theme

Meanwhile, your math teacher gets a letter from a prestigious math summer program and immediately thinks of you. You get nominated with a stellar letter of support and end up getting into the program.

Throughout your data science internship, you realize how few minorities are represented in the field. This is something you care about, so you decide to put together a panel so that more students in your community could learn about this profession. You make sure to reach out to the cultural clubs on campus to increase attendance.

Your event was a success, and students email you asking when the next event is. You decide to form a data science club that puts on conferences and talks to spread awareness of this career.

Step 6 - Validate your credibility

You contact your local newspaper and they say they would love to help you. At the end of junior year, you prep and score high on your SATs. When you apply to college, you are a standout applicant. You have a strong data science theme with activities that relate to it, your teachers and your data science mentor write letters of recommendation that wow, and you send in your newspaper article about the conference and its impact.

Step 7- Earn your Target SAT / ACT score

You take both practice tests and score way higher on the ACT. You study for 2 months and get your target score of 35/36.

You get into MIT, Princeton, and many other great schools!

Summary

* In step 6 of ACHIEVE, you learned that your passion portfolio is going to be judged by admissions officers based on the level of passion and impact that you display.
* This chapter gave you some tips for increasing the impact of your project, such as by using social media and pitching your project to local/online publications.
* Finally, you learned how to rewrite your resume or profile bullet points with result + action to make sure the reader understands the impact that you've achieved.

Action Steps

- [ ] Brainstorm 3 ways that you increase your impact and bolster your credibility
- [ ] Pitch 5 local publications or magazines related to your project
- [ ] Keep track of your accomplishments every semester by writing your resume bullets using result + action

CHAPTER 12

β

Step 7 of ACHIEVE - Earn your target SAT/ACT score

Congratulations, you made it to the last step of ACHIEVE! By now, you've gotten into the toughest classes you can while focusing on a specific subject and keeping up grades in your core courses. You've gotten to know your teachers and had them sign up to be your club's mentor, or your personal mentor, and you've found and reached out to other mentors and professionals for informational interviews. You started working on a passion project or internship that showcases your curiosity in a certain industry, you've gotten third-party validation for your project, and now, the last step is to earn that SAT/ACT target score that will seal your spot in your dream college.

Earning it means that you have to study. There's just no way around it, unless you were born to take standardized tests. If you aren't a natural test-taker (like I'm not), there are ways to make it easier and more time efficient. This chapter will go into why standardized test scores are important and give you some strategies you can apply to get your target score.

The SAT/ACT dread

I hated standardized testing. The only thing I enjoyed from the experience was that my name was short and took less time to bubble than the rest of my class. Now, I know it's natural to dislike things you're not great at, such as standardized test taking. Unlike my peers in my honors and AP classes, I got an embarrassingly low score the first time I took the SAT. Even though I didn't prepare for the SAT, I thought I was at least going to get a 2000 out of 2400 (based on the old scale) like my friends.

Nope, I scored a good few hundred points lower. I was in denial for a bit, but then I decided to not let the score define me. I want to help others beat the college admissions test because it shouldn't define you either.

The importance of these tests

"SAT and ACT scores represent your college readiness." What does this really mean? Colleges still use standardized testing because, according to the College Board, it is a "common standard" that all schools can agree on in order to rank students from all over the world and all high schools.

This is one of the main ways for admissions officers to understand your standing relative to other students in your high school and how rigorous your high school really is. If the average student at your school is taking 5 AP classes, then anything less than that would be seen as not keeping up with your peers. It also gets tricky around grade inflation, the tendency for some schools to be less rigorous than others. Such is the case when in High School A, everyone gets As while at High School B, very few students get As per class. It seems that in this case, High School B has a more difficult program.

The "college readiness" of admitted students also matters to colleges because graduation and retention rates affect their ranking in the U.S. News "Best Colleges" list. Recently, however, testing scandals and research have prompted 1000+ colleges to go test optional. Bob Schaeffer, director of a nonprofit called FairTest, said:[17]

"Combined with the University of Chicago's decision to go test-optional . . . and the University of California's review of its use of the ACT/SAT, there's no question that the still-unfolding scandal will lead more higher education institutions to drop their ACT/SAT testing requirements."

Nonetheless, nonprofits like Student Research Foundation believe that the ACT and SAT won't go away, since those that do well on these tests (a lot of Harvard applicants) will continue to take them. For now, you should plan on studying for a high score on either the ACT or SAT.

Why should you care about a higher score?

I asked myself this question a lot. I believed my academic transcript showed that I could excel in college. However, colleges are more competitive than ever. More international applicants and the ease of online applications have driven down admission rates at Harvard and other top colleges. Today, Harvard's acceptance rate is about half what it was ten years ago.[18]

As colleges get more competitive, things such as grades, the SAT, ACT, and APs become a benchmark to get in. In other words, if you don't meet the college's score range, then you are likely to be denied

---

[17] https://www.iacac.org/wp-content/uploads/2014/05/H59-Defining-Promise.pdf

[18] https://www.statista.com/statistics/936539/ivy-league-harvard-university-acceptance-rate-class/

admission (even if on paper your desired school says they are "test-optional").

Of course, there are other things like extracurriculars, your essays, and recommendations to consider, but when you have so many competitive applicants (with high scores), it's easy to get passed over when you have low test scores. Don't let this be you. These tests are manageable. Just like you don't expect to get a strike the first time you bowl, a high test score can require some practice.

First, pick one test — the ACT or SAT

Take the official ACT and SAT practice tests and see how you do. Pick the test that you do better at and commit to practicing. Personally, I did much better on the ACT than the SAT with no practice, so I picked the ACT. If that's not for you, just pick the one you like most or dislike the least.

Then, set your target score

I would recommend pulling out your list of "reach colleges." "Reach colleges" are colleges that have admission rates lower than 10% if your stats (grades, test scores) are below their average.

Then, look up the test score range for the college. For example, Harvard's ACT range is 33–35, meaning that if you get a 35 you will be above average.[19] While it is possible to get in with a 32, a below-average score for Harvard, I suggest you aim for the 75th percentile or the 35. Harvard's SAT range is 1460-1570, so aim for 1570 if you are taking the SAT. There are always special circumstances such as legacies (your

---

[19] https://oir.harvard.edu/files/huoir/files/harvard_cds_2019-2020.pdf

parents attended that college), sports recruits, or other special talented admits that may skew the test range lower.

"Shoot for the moon. Even if you miss, you'll land among the stars." Norman Vincent Peale

Practice, review, practice

You will be taking a lot of practice tests and reviewing your answers, then practicing more. I think I completed 50+ exams. With each exam, you get better, faster, and more confident.

For the most effective practice, make sure you are practicing the sections you can improve the most in. For example, if you are weaker in the math section, focus on that section first. It's much easier to raise your ACT score from a 27 to a 30 rather than 30 to 33.

The most important thing is to review the wrong answers and write out what you learned. Compile this learning in one place and review it every time you practice. This way, every failure makes you wiser. Take the full-length exam at least every week so you can practice your endurance and stamina. Make sure to time yourself.

Consistent score = success

When will you be ready for the real deal? If you keep getting your goal score consistently, then I would go ahead and take the real exam. Keep in mind that some test prep books vary in difficulty from the real exam, so try to take as many official exams as possible. I found that Barron's Test Prep was harder, so I would score lower, and McGraw-Hill's Test Prep was easier, so my score would be inflated. One book that helped me get a high score was Barron's ACT 36. It teaches you the tactics to get as close as possible to a perfect score. I liked the way it was written for high-achievers, and the strategies improved my testing approach.

After all those practice tests, I not only scored far better, I actually started to enjoy the test. All of this was through practice. I didn't let my first score define me or limit me from admission to Harvard. I decided it was worth it to keep trying, learn from my failures, and do my best on exam day.

As *Harry Potter* author J.K. Rowling said:

"It is impossible to live without failing at something, unless you live so cautiously that you might as well not have lived at all — in which case, you fail by default."

Your hard work and dedication will pay off. Even if you sucked at standardized test scores, your perseverance will reap you rewards beyond a high score. You've got this!

Skill: the accountability buddy

Don't have an accountability buddy? You should.

My accountability buddy motivated me to publish my first article. She also pushed me to exercise more and strategize how to get to early retirement. I finally made meditation a habit because of my accountability buddy. It might be crazy to think that having an accountability partner could have so many advantages, but stick with me. Here's a few it gave me.

1. I Learned To Coach Myself

When you have an accountability partner, you are responsible for setting your goals and figuring out how to achieve them. Yes, you can bounce ideas off of your partner, but that person is not your coach. Your partner keeps you accountable for results rather than just the "how."

An example goal with my accountability partner would be to record 8-10 TikToks per week. Yours might be to study the Math section of your SAT practice book. You keep each other accountable by meeting up every week and discussing what can help you get to your goals. Two heads are always better than one, I'm told.

By learning to coach yourself, you become more resourceful in figuring out the route to your intended result—one of the most important skills you can learn. You learn quickly if you have a system (besides your check-ins) that helps you follow through, like turning your weekly goal into a daily goal and scheduling it.

2. I Learned to Prioritize the Most Important Task

After several weeks of failing to meet my goals and talking to my accountability partner about it, we devised a strategy to prioritize my tasks so that I could make the most important goal happen.

The strategy is great, but what really unlocked my potential was being able to manage my time effectively. Google Calendar tasks became my life. I loved the color coding and intricacies of making all these things work.

But how do you know what to prioritize? Here lies the ultimate question. I would recommend that you lean into your strengths and go really deep and specific. Most of the students I met at Harvard had something very unique that they put all their heart and soul into while at high school. Whether that is playing piano at an international level or generating significant funds for charitable causes, Ivy League students show focus in a given field.

When you lean into your strengths, you will make faster progress. Using my strength of curiosity, I asked a lot of questions that led me to find my career direction, advisors, and internships. Thinking about your goals in relation to your strengths will make unrelated tasks easy to avoid. It will become instinctual for you to plan and prioritize based on your strengths.

3. I Strengthened Friendships

I chose two friends to keep me accountable and now we are closer than ever. We know what one another is doing and provide mutual support. We share resources, introductions, and events.

The benefits don't stop there. Studies show strong social connections lead to greater pain tolerance, a stronger immune system, and a lower risk of depression and early death.

According to behavior expert Dr. Patrick Wanis, relationships are strengthened by quality time, but in order to have that, you need to have quantity of time. Having weekly or bi-weekly check-ins will strengthen your friendships.

It's hard to stay in touch when we are all so busy. But helping each other reach goals provides you more reasons to stay connected. Are you ready to reach your goals and reap these rewards?

ACHIEVE in action - Government example

Let's imagine your dream career is to do something in government and public policy. You go to a public school that only has an AP government class for one semester. You also don't know anyone in government, so that's not helping you either.

Step 1 - Aim for As in Advanced Classes

First, you make sure to turn in some missing assignments for your honors math course and ask your friend to speak Spanish with you to help you study for the next exam. Once you get these grades to a comfortable position, you move on to the next step.

Step 2 - Conduct an Activity Audit

You have so many interests and you enjoy almost everything. However, you realize that even if you got an internship with a senator, you wouldn't have the time to do it, so you commit to the Activity Audit and cancel your memberships in choir, band, and your school newspaper.

Step 3 - Help your Teacher Help You

You now have some time to work on special projects with your government teacher. Over time, you become friends and find out that he knows people in the local city government.

Step 4 - Ignite your Interests

You ask your teacher to introduce you and he sets up a call for you with a City Council member.

You craft well-researched questions and impress the city council member. At the end of the call, you ask about opportunities for you to get involved. She shares with you that the city youth council is about to close applications in a week and shares the details of how to apply.

Step 5 - Execute your Theme

You apply and get an interview. Because of your research and your enthusiastic personality, they admit you to the City Council youth board.

On the Council, you meet a mentor who takes you under her wing and introduces you to her peer whom she went to college with and happens to be a senator. He happens to be hiring for interns and you get one of the spots. You get selected to join the marketing team that gets out the vote.

You do such a great job that you get nominated and have a personal recommendation from a senator to do a prestigious internship at the White House. Your internship was nothing like you thought it was going to be. But you make the most out of it and write a blog about the dark side of the White House.

Step 6 - Validate your Credibility

One of your articles gets picked up at a popular online blog. After junior summer, you decide to buckle down and drill the SATs.

Step 7 - Earn your Target SAT / ACT score

At first, you are scoring super low and feeling overwhelmed by the exam. However, you keep going with your daily practice and hire a tutor to help. With your hard work and dedication and some help, you get your target SAT score.

When you apply to colleges, you make sure to include a snippet of your article in the blog. You also highlight your theme of government and write about your desire and actions to affect policy in your city throughout your application.

Future Ivy

You stand out and get admitted to Georgetown, Princeton, and many other top schools.

Summary

* In step 7 of ACHIEVE, you learned that the SAT/ACT standardized tests scores are a crucial part of your application to indicate that you are ready for their college level classes.
* You learned how to figure out your target score by taking the 75th percentile of the range, and you learned how to study for the exam.
* Finally, you learned one of my favorite skills: the accountability buddy system. There is nothing better than having a friend go through all of this with you.

Action Steps

- ☐ Schedule one full practice exam per week for at least 8 weeks
- ☐ Analyze your wrong answers and write out what you would do next time
- ☐ Find an accountability partner and meet weekly

Future Ivy

Part 3

Σ

Implementation of ACHIEVE

Future Ivy

CHAPTER 13

Σ

Putting it all together

Now that you know the 7 skills that will help you through ACHIEVE, you have to put them to use. Like instruments in an orchestra, you have to learn to play them harmoniously. Don't worry, practice makes perfect, and you know I'm here with some tips. This section of the book contains skills and resources that will help you implement all the skills in unison.

With a better understanding of the ACHIEVE system, you can set out to put it in action. This really applies to any career and interest out there. ACHIEVE is arranged in chronological order, as in worry about A before V, but you will often find yourself jumping around and reusing the skills you've learned in earlier steps. For example, I recommend that you do your "activities audit" every month or so, in multiple of the steps. I also recommend you use the techniques from cold emailing and getting to know your teachers simultaneously and often.

You can also remember ACHIEVE when you get lost or don't know where you are in the process. Just fill in the blanks and know that it's never too late. Even if you're reading this during your senior year, with the right motivation and work ethic, you can absolutely nail the ACHIEVE system and set yourself up for success.

Think of ACHIEVE as the tools you need to build a house. With each tool, there are tasks and skills to master, but using the right tool makes the job much easier. But hang on, even if you have all the tools and the skills and the whatnot, you still need a master blueprint with instructions, right?

When you pick a project that truly interests you, you will be motivated to execute it. But you may quickly be shut down by the realities of the project. "Is this even possible? Can I really do this?" All these questions will pop up and make you doubt yourself. The truth is, no one has a master blueprint for your life; you have to create it yourself. That being said, sometimes a little guidance and accountability can help a ton.

Your "why" as your guide

In chapter 4, you brainstormed your "why" and narrowed it down. This chapter will help you revisit your "why" and make it more solid. Your "why" is your secret reserve. It's the fuel that keeps you going when you are drained and it is crucial for getting things done.

Your "why" needs to be emotionally charged. It needs to bring you to tears (if crying comes easily). For me, it was all about creating a better life for my future family. I grew up in a chaotic household full of arguments, hot tempers, and dysfunction. I not only wanted to get out, but I now want to help others escape and create a better life. I wanted to inspire others to become confident public speakers and be aware of current events. I wanted to inspire the future leaders at my school.

When you start focusing on your "why" and how your project will help others, it can help you overcome your fears and doubts. For example, maybe you have a big speech in front of the school board to change the class schedule to be more in line with teenager sleep schedules. Focusing on the kids you will help with this change will help you override your fear of public speaking. Also know that when you are doing things that are outside of your comfort zone, like starting a new club, it helps you grow as a person. This is one thing colleges are looking for when they rate your personal qualities.

Focusing on your "why" will also help you make tough decisions in life. Let's say your goal is to become a biomechanical engineer, and you have a choice between attending a biomed conference hosted by NASA or a high-profile Supreme Court case. If you were passionate about Law, then you would probably choose to experience a Supreme Court case decision. It all depends on the lens you are using to make your decision through. Remember your "why" often, and you'll be able to make more confident decisions.

The "Heaven exercise"

Whether you are religious or not, bear with me for an exercise that can help you discover your personal mission.

First close your eyes and imagine that you are dead in Heaven (dramatic, I know, but stay with me here :)). Imagine that God is there and reciting all your accomplishments. You have your best friends, mentors, and loved ones next to you. What type of accomplishments is God reciting?

For example, Bob imagines that God is reciting that he helped his local community prosper by campaigning for small business-friendly policies and helping teens get employed at these small businesses. He served as a mentor for these teens and helped them figure out their career paths and what colleges would help them the most, whether that was a community college or an Ivy.

Maybe you discover that you have a desire to increase literacy rates in so-called "bad" neighborhoods in your area and fundraise for public libraries to be built in those areas. Because of that, more youth have a safe place to do school work. Because of that, some of the students start to believe in themselves and apply for college. Because of that, they end up finding out that they qualify for a full-ride scholarship. Because of that, they graduate from college with no debt, get a high-paying job, and break the cycle of poverty.

"Without a mission statement, you may get to the top of the ladder and then realize it was leaning against the wrong building," said Dave Ramsey.

Ikigai

Ikigai is a Japanese concept of finding your purpose. "Iki" stands for "life" and "gai" stands for "worth."[20] Together, your Ikigai, what makes your life worth living, or "reason for being" lies at the intersection of these 4 questions:

1. What do you love to do?
2. What are you good at?
3. What can you get paid to do?
4. What does the world need?

Maybe you love cooking, sewing, and reading. You are good at chemistry and being patient while you teach your friends the chemistry concepts. Your Ikigai might be to take complex scientific concepts and teach them in easy-to-understand ways, like with cooking.

Jane Goodall, a famous primatologist, loved working with apes and gained expertise over years of working with them, developing a

---

[20] https://positivepsychology.com/ikigai/

career by publishing books and speaking publicly. Her ikigai could be protecting and furthering our knowledge of the great apes.

To put this concept into practice, take out a sheet of paper and create a list for each of the 4 questions. What do you see as the intersection of these questions? Let your excitement guide you.

Time

In order to have a successful project, you also need the time to execute it. If you are overwhelmed with your classes and activities, go back to Step 2 to conduct an activities audit and cut out unnecessary ones.

It's better to do a little each day to get the momentum going, but it's okay to also spend a few hours on the weekend instead. In order to create the most impact in getting your project started, focus on the most important task. When I was starting the debate club, the most important first task was getting the club registered and then recruiting members for the first meeting. Write down the milestones and set a deadline so you can work toward it. Ask your mentor or friends to keep you accountable for the milestones you set.

Goal-getting 101

"You hit every single goal last year?" I said with surprise.

"Yes, it happens every year. I frame my goals and look at them every day," my accountability partner and high achieving friend told me.

I felt a tinge of "not being good enough," as I had only accomplished a few of my goals last year, but I wanted to "be better" instead of "feeling better," so I investigated how my high achieving friend did it. I'll share with you lessons I've learned from the most ambitious and successful people I know.

What you and I probably know about goal-setting isn't working. Every new year, thousands of people set New Year's resolutions, yet at the end of the year, or even in February, the resolution becomes forgotten about and left behind. One of the reasons is because no one has taught you how to set better, "more achievable" goals. Even if you know how to set goals, common knowledge is not the same as common practice.

First, let's review the basics. I like the goal framework of S.M.A.R.T.E.R. goals.[21]

S.M.A.R.T.E.R. goals

- S - Specific, can you measure it?
- M - Meaningful, does it connect with your "why"?
- A - Achievable, is this a goal that you have control of?
- R - Relevant, does this goal connect what you want out of life?
- T - Time-bound, what's your deadline?
- E - Evaluate, how often are you visiting your goals?
- R - Readjust, does this goal still serve me? Should I adjust my approach?

For every goal you set, run through the letters and questions to maximize your chance of achieving them.

There are 4 big things that I've seen in my friends that achieve all their goals. The first one is how often they review their goals. The more

---

[21] https://www.wanderlustworker.com/setting-s-m-a-r-t-e-r-goals-7-steps-to-achieving-any-goal/

I've seen a friend review their goals, the more likely they achieve them. I mentioned earlier, but one of my friends has a frame of all her goals that she reviews every morning. My other friend who has achieved all her goals has a goal-tracking sheet that she is reviewing three times a day. I started reviewing my goals more often and have seen more progress, since I keep them top of mind.

The second thing that separates goal-setters from goal-getters is how big of a goal they set. This falls into the achievable category or question. For example, writing a book is a big and daunting project, but when you break it down into different components, like first you will brainstorm the book, then you will outline it, then you will write the first draft, this will make the goal easier to achieve. Creating bite-sized goals will reduce the fear of starting as well.

The third thing to do is schedule your goals. To make a goal happen, you need to know when you will work on it and where you will achieve it. For example, you might schedule and follow through with doing SAT practice tests every Saturday morning 9am-12pm in your basement, where there is a desk with a timer and the material is all ready for you.

The last thing I noticed was that accountability can help you reach your goals. If you wanted to do SAT prep every Saturday, maybe you could ask your mom to remind you or wake you up in the morning. Maybe you do it with a friend every week over video chat. Involve people who are disciplined and you will also become more disciplined with your goals.

The most important thing is to get started, so what's one small step you can take to start your goals?

Summary

- In this chapter, you learned that the ACHIEVE system can help you figure out where you are in the process and where to focus next.
- You also learned some exercises that can help you revisit your "why," because having a clear "why" helps you make the right decisions when you face a challenge or doubt.
- Finally, you learned the difference between "goal-setters" and "goal-getters" and how you can join the latter group through tools like S.M.A.R.T.E.R. goals.

Action Steps

- ☐ Refer back to the ACHIEVE system often, as it gives helpful tools that you can apply to other aspects of your life
- ☐ Use the framework of SMARTER goals to make sure you stay motivated
- ☐ Describe a clear "why" for your journey

Future Ivy

CHAPTER 14

Σ

Building a team

You have a tough job as a student. You not only have loads of homework and exams to study for but also clubs and extracurriculars to manage. Not to mention getting enough sleep, hanging out with the fam, and having a social life. So, how do you do it all? Well, you need a team.

When I was president of my school health club HOSA, I had a lot of help from my club officers and members. My mission was to make the conference free to attend for all members by focusing on fundraising.

I got help from the team in brainstorming fundraising ideas. With those ideas, we put on three big fundraisers. The first was gift wrapping at our local shopping mall. During Christmas, shoppers would have us wrap their gifts and donate money to our club. Each member signed up for a different shift so we had all the busy days covered.

During the year, we did a See's Candies fundraiser where each member was tasked with selling one box of chocolates. And in the spring, we did Jamba Juice fundraisers where we had our members pitch in a shift or two. We also applied for grants with the help of our club advisor.

Together as a team, our club was able to raise enough money to go to the conference without any money out of their pocket. It was amazing to know that no one was going to be limited by their financial situation and we were all going to the conference together.

If it was just me, I highly doubt we would have had this success. I experienced the same thing when I started the debate team. Some members pitched in their homes for us to practice. Other members offered to drive us to the tournaments. You can get more done when you have a team. Plus it can make the work more fun, especially if you involve your friends.

Your team's size

A team can be as small as you and your friend or it could be a big, 30+-member club. They can help you brainstorm ways to get you closer to your vision and help execute your plans. They also can help you from becoming overwhelmed.

You should start assembling your team once you have a clear purpose, like helping students improve their public speaking skills or helping to normalize mental health issues. Once you have the purpose, you can recruit members who also believe in the same purpose and who want to do something about it. When you start building your team, it's good to have specific roles so your members know how they can help and can interview for those roles. You can look to other club positions for inspiration. For example, the secretary can help you make sure meetings are scheduled and notes are taken. Your treasurer can help create the fundraising budget. You might have a social media person establish your social presence.

Lay out all the roles and descriptions you need and then start interviewing.

Recruiting

To get applicants, use your personal network of friends but also ask for referrals from friends of anyone who is passionate about the cause. If your school has a school club day or a newsletter, that might be a good spot to advertise. At most high schools, there is a procedure to get your club registered. Ask your guidance counselor about the process. Usually you'll need a teacher as an advisor to the club and a club charter - what the club is about.

When interviewing, you can use a Google form to collect basic info such as how they found out about the club and why they are interested, then schedule an interview to dig deep on their communication, enthusiasm, and ability to collaborate.

Team meetings

Once you finalize your team, you'll want to schedule a regular meeting full of inspiration and ice breakers. After that meeting, involve your team members in your plans so that they feel motivated to stick with the club. People prefer to act if they feel like they came up with the idea themselves.

It's important to bring the team together to brainstorm and then have them vote on the ideas they want to follow through on. You'll notice more participation when you've involved them.

Another example of involving your team is to help them stay updated on important things related to the club like if you just applied for a grant or got a club feature in the local newspaper.

Sometimes you'll have members that aren't a good fit. Whether they are overcommitted or just flaky, it happens, and you might be frustrated and rightfully angry. However, if you want your club or project to succeed, you need to focus on retaining your club members that are a good fit.

Advisors

Another important part of your team is its advisors. You can think of them as mentors as well, but basically this is anyone that can help you if you get stuck. For example, you are starting a new club at school and have to get a teacher to be involved. If they're helping you by answering your questions, then they are mentoring you! You can get your favorite teachers involved, or you can look outside of school for career-specific mentors.

I would recommend having a mentor to keep you on track and to advise you. Ask people like your high school counselor, teacher, or local professional if they could be available when you have questions on this project. They can help provide advice if you hit roadblocks and later on write you a letter of recommendation for college applications.

The project that I picked was starting the debate team at my high school. I asked my high school counselor about the process to start a club and then filled out all the necessary paperwork. I then asked Mr. L, who helped me get my law internship, to be the club's advisor.

I scheduled the first meeting and started to recruit members. A lot of fear and insecurity will come up when you start something new. You may start wondering, "Will people show up?" or "What if this will be an utter failure?" What helped me get through was focusing on my "why." Why did I want to start the debate team?

Summary

- In this chapter, you learned that nobody expects you to go through this process alone.
- It's a lot of work and you'll need some help, so I recommend you set up a team that can help you.
- This team can include your friends to help you brainstorm activities, your family for moral support, and various teachers or professionals that can advise you along the way.

Action Steps

- ☐ Lay out all the roles and descriptions of what you need on your team
- ☐ Find an advisor for your club/project
- ☐ Recruit your team

Part 4

Ω

The College Application

The last part of this book deals with everything that goes into the actual college application. The specific requirements will vary slightly from school to school, but the major principles apply to all. You will learn how to look at your application from the perspective of the admissions department, how to choose and write personal essays that show your impact, and finally how to put everything together and nail your college interviews.

Future Ivy

CHAPTER 15

Ω

What we know about Ivy League admissions

We've actually learned a lot about the super-secret Ivy League admission process in the past few years that can help you better understand the admissions decisions. This chapter will cover what has been discovered and what the common dataset, admissions websites, and the Harvard lawsuit mean for you.

The common dataset

Getting into an Ivy League is like being an elite athlete in academics and passion. Just like an elite athlete, you need to prioritize your time and what's most important, for example SAT prep vs. extracurriculars.

What's most important? The common dataset, a collaborative effort among schools to improve college admission data, has some of the answers. These datasets are publicly available on Google, and each college releases their own data so that the higher education community can better understand the process.

After you find the common dataset for the school you are interested in, you'll find a super long pdf file. The section you want to search for is the "How admissions makes decisions and the relative importance" of factors in admission decisions. This section lists several academic and non-academic factors, such as the relative importance of

Future Ivy

the interview or your GPA. If you want a video tutorial, check it out in the free video course at the end of this book.

For example, if you look up "UPenn common dataset," you'll see a chart highlighting that the "essay" and "rigor" of your classes are "very important," whereas your "class rank" is only "important."[22] You will also see that "character and personal qualities" are very important and which I will explain later in this chapter.

You'll also see for UPenn that they do consider your "interest" in the school. For example, if Bob had networked with a UPenn professor in high school and done research with her, then that student would stand out to UPenn versus a student who has made no attempt to research or attend the university.

Schools want to know "why our school?" just as they want your application to tell them "why you?" Some schools like Yale or Cornell say they don't consider your interest level, but I believe it will still help you stand out.

Now that you've learned about this data, look up your top three dream schools and look up what they rate as most important in their decision to admit you. You'll see that many of the Ivies have something in common: "academics" are important but "personal qualities" are where you can stand out!

Some examples of "personal qualities"

- Selflessness
- Humility
- Resilience

---

[22] https://www.upenn.edu/ir/Common%20Data%20Set/UPenn-Common-Data-Set-2019-20.pdf?pdf=CDS%202019-20

- Judgement
- Citizenship
- Spirit and camaraderie with peers

This means that when you're writing your essays and interviewing, you'll want to highlight some of these qualities in your character and experience in order to show that you've done your research.

Admissions website

If you are applying for an internship, you probably want to learn more about the company before sending in your application, right? Where would you look for more info? Their website, of course! The same applies to your dream school.

I'll walk you through two examples: Harvard and Columbia. On Harvard's website, they write that they are looking for the "individuals who will inspire those around them during their college years and beyond."[23] One of the Ivy League students I interviewed showed this quality. He went abroad to study microfinance and then became passionate about it, so he started a publication to increase awareness and teach his peers.

Next, Harvard breaks down 4 categories of things that they look for:

- Growth and potential - Are you stretching yourself to capacity? Do you have a direction?
- Interest and activities - Do you deeply care about your activities? What impact have you had?

---

[23] https://college.harvard.edu/admissions/apply/what-we-look

- Personal character - Do you consider yourself calm under pressure, mature, humorous, caring, or open-minded?
- Contribution to Harvard community - Will you contribute to Harvard and will Harvard help you?

If Harvard is your dream school, I would reflect on where you stand with respect to these categories and what you can do to improve your standing in each. For example, you can show your growth and potential by making the most of the resources available to you. This can include taking all of the advanced classes at school and maybe even some at the local community college. They will check into your past behavior to see how you've contributed to your community. Top schools see your behavior in high school as a good predictor of your future, so if you contributed significantly to your community, there is a good chance that you'll continue to do this.

Each school has different qualities they are looking for based on the culture they are trying to create, so make sure that your application materials are tailored to that school. For Columbia, they are looking for "curious thinkers" who would be a good fit for the urban campus life, since it is in New York City.[24] On the University of Pennsylvania (UPenn) admission website, they bring up that they value students who "emulate their founder Benjamin Franklin by applying their knowledge in service to society."[25]

The Harvard lawsuit

In 2014, an organization called "Students for Admissions" sued Harvard claiming that they discriminated against Asian Americans. Five

---

[24] https://undergrad.admissions.columbia.edu/apply/first-year/holistic
[25] https://admissions.upenn.edu/admissions-and-financial-aid/what-penn-looks-for

years later, the courts ruled in favor of Harvard that the admission process doesn't unduly discriminate against Asian Americans.[26]

Because of this case, there were a lot of things that were released to the public about Harvard's secret admission process. Having insight into how your admissions officer reads your file will help you understand how to stand out to your dream school.

For example, when your application is received, it's divided into geographic areas based on your high school's address.[27] Then, it gets sent to the subcommittee with a senior admissions officer and 3-6 other admissions officers. The first admissions officer that reviews your application gives your application a 1-4 rating, with 1 being the best. There is an overall rating, then an academic rating, extracurricular, athletic, personal, and letter of support rating.

The Application Rating System

Here's an example of Harvard's rating system. 1-4 rating, where 1 is the best, with 5-6 for special circumstances like family responsibilities.

The Academic Rating

The Academic Rating is determined by the following factors: grades, standardized test scores, letters of recommendation, academic prizes, submitted academic work, and the strength of applicants' high school.

---

[26] https://admissionscase.harvard.edu/lawsuit
[27] https://admissionscase.harvard.edu/files/adm-case/files/2019-10-30_dkt_672_findings_of_fact_and_conclusions_of_law.pdf

Future Ivy

What does each number mean?

1- genuine scholar, near-perfect grades and scores, unusual creativity
2- superb grades, mid-to-high 700 SAT, ACT 33+
3- excellent grades, mid 600-low 700, ACT 29-32
4- respectable grades, low-to-mid 600 SAT, ACT 26-29

The Extracurriculars Rating

To figure out your extracurricular rating, your admissions officer will consider your activity list, your letters of recommendation, awards, and potentially your essay (depending on what you write about).

What does each number mean?

1- national level, professional, truly unusual achievement
2- local, regional level, strong contributor to high school like class president
3- solid participation
4- little participation

The Letter of Recommendation rating

Personal qualities that are more subjective, such as what others say about you, can go into your rating. There can also be special family circumstances that you can mention in your interview or essays that show qualities of maturity. Some qualities that admissions officers may look for in your file include:

- Courage in the face of seemingly insurmountable obstacles
- Leadership
- Sincerity

What does each number mean?

1- strikingly unusual support, "the best I've seen in my career"

2- strong support, "one of the best"

3- above average support

4- neutral, slightly negative support

The Athletic Rating

Harvard has an athletic rating. You can get in without playing sports, so don't worry if you are a 4 on this one like I was.

What does each number mean?

1- recruited athlete
2- strong contribution, possible leadership roles
3- active participation
4- little or no participation

Overall rating

You also get an overall rating, like your GPA, and it factors in all the details from your application. If you get a 1, then the officer thinks you are a "clear admit." Your application then might go to a second admissions officer and be discussed in the docket subcommittee group.

Other colleges like Dartmouth might have a 1-9 scale, but the process is similar.[28] You have to make the best impression in the few minutes that your first admissions officer has your file. You must win them over with your passion, story, and mission.

---

[28] *A Is for Admission: The Insider's Guide to Getting into the Ivy League and Other Top Colleges* by Michele A. Hernández

Future Ivy

Summary

* In this chapter, you learned about the "common dataset" and how you can use publicly available info, provided by your dream college, to increase your chances of an acceptance decision.
* You also learned how schools like Harvard rate your application and what you can be doing to get the admissions officer to write "clear admit" on your application.

Action Steps

- ☐ Review where you are on the ratings
- ☐ Brainstorm ways to improve
- ☐ Look up your top 3 schools' common dataset's "relative importance" section

CHAPTER 16

Ω

College essays

What admissions officers are looking for and what to avoid

According to the former assistant director of admission at Dartmouth, the essays can help your application reader understand your motivation, "what kind of person you are" (hint, hint) your "personal qualities," and how well you write and think.[29] Since admissions officers already have your academic record and activity list, tell them a story that is not otherwise in your application and showcases your personal qualities.

For example, say Sally loves to go bowling with her family but her family doesn't live close to the bowling alley, so she invents a new game like bowling but with cans and creates a neighborhood league. When a local business owner is inspired and wants to put in a bowling alley in town, she works with Sally to make sure there is a space for her budding community. This shows how passionate Sally is, how she is a problem solver vs. a complainer, and that she is a leader in her community.

Another example is a student named Bob who loves gardening and sustainable agriculture. His family loves to garden and he grew up planting, weeding, and learning about soil. His passion is related to eco-

---

[29] *A Is for Admission: The Insider's Guide to Getting into the Ivy League and Other Top Colleges* by Michele A. Hernández

friendly agriculture techniques specifically in reforming pesticides. He started off by doing online research and then started to attend conferences. He then started a website with other friends who were interested in the same topic. He started a podcast that gave tips for local farmers. Soon, he gained an audience and was invited to speak at local events for horticulturists. He then started consulting for small farms and presenting with his team at agricultural fairs. A local environmental activist reached out and got Bob featured in the local newspaper.

In his essay, he might mention how privileged he was to have the experience, showing his humility. He also might use his story to show his ability to collaborate and set up a team. If your admissions officer can read your essay and get a sense of what type of roommate you'll be, or at least want to get to know you, then you did your job.

Another useful tactic you can use is the "Swap Test." If you change your name to some other random person at your school, would the essay still fit? Or is it unique to you? Strive to tell your own story so that you stand out.

Cliche topics

There are a few things to avoid: cliche topics and topics that reflect poorly on you. Some cliche topics include:

- Outward bound essay - how you survived the elements
- Community service essay - how you realized that people from different backgrounds are actually the same
- Death of grandparents essay - you don't want people to feel sorry for you
- The big sport game - unless you are a recruited athlete

In fact, avoid the 3 Ds as a college essay topic: Death, Depression, Divorce. You also want to avoid topics that might reflect poorly on you, like issues with drugs, breakups, or your anger problems. We all have things we should work on, but your college essay is about marketing yourself rather than revealing your downsides.

Why you should care about essays

"Rawr!" I ran after my little sister while pretending to be a lion. My little sister ran around our kitchen island trying to avoid being devoured.

I used to love scaring my family members, especially when I was 8 and spritely enough to sneak around and jump out to startle my victims. One day, though, I scared my mom so badly that she dropped a plate of cookies and made it rain chocolate chips.

While shaking her finger at me, she told me that when she was my age, she loved to scare people just as much as I did. Until one day, she scared her elderly neighbor so badly that she had a heart attack and died. I was shocked and told myself that I didn't want to kill anyone. That night, my trickster phase ended and nothing has been the same. Sad.

But wait, there's more. Years later, I learned from my sister that my mom had lied to me to try to teach me a lesson! Can you believe that? I'm just saying that you can't play with me like that, mom. Scaring people was all I had in the world as an 8 year old.

So, why am I sharing this with you when we are talking about college essays? Think back to the best teachers you've had. Did they splurt out a bunch of facts, or did they put it into a story?

What do you remember more between facts and stories?

If you said stories, that's because humans are wired for stories. They are sticky, and the more details you can add, the more immersive your story will feel.

If you look up the common dataset for your dream school, you will have found that most top schools rank your "personal statement" as "very important."

You also may have found that "personal qualities" rate as "very important" as well. Use this to your advantage and share a story in your essay that expresses your personal qualities while getting the admissions officer to root for you!

For example, if you wanted to express your strength of creativity, you might describe how you started a movement during quarantine to stay connected with your friends, or you could write about how you stepped up and found a job to support your family when your dad got laid off, showcasing your maturity.

Essays are one of the best ways to stand out because you get many tries. My debate coach always said, "there is no good writing, only good rewriting." You have control over the stories you tell, so remember that the goal is to get the admissions officers to root for you.

Ivy League admission factors

If you look up UPenn admission factors and their relative importance, you might observe that most of the academic stuff is rated as "very important." This is because they want to make sure that you are able to succeed at the Ivy League level, and the majority of the people that apply are qualified.

Something that might be surprising to you is that "character" and "personal qualities" are rated as "very important." Yes, it's on the same level as "academics," because college is as much a social experience as well as academic, and they're looking for people who are going to be good roommates. Schools such as Yale or Cornell also list the "application essay" as "very important." You can use the essay to communicate your "character" and "personal qualities."

Types of essays

There are a few types of essays in the college admission process. The main essay is called your "application essay" or "personal statement." This is the essay that you submit with the Common Application, which is where you will likely submit your applications.

The other type of essay is the "supplemental essay." These essay topics will vary from college to college. The goal of the "supplemental essay," according to Richard Nesbitt, director of admissions at Williams College, is to understand your values and what "makes you tick."[30]

Here are some examples. Dartmouth has a supplement that asks: "What attracts you to Dartmouth?"[31] Princeton asks you to write about your "commitment to service and civic engagement."[32] Harvard asks you to write 150 words on "one of your extracurricular activities or work experiences."[33] The topics may vary, but the goal is still the same: you

---

[30] https://www.bostonglobe.com/metro/regionals/2015/10/30/don-just-write-off-that-supplemental-essay/CsJeIWF8ZKcQ9d8i5lMQ4I/story.html

[31] https://admissions.dartmouth.edu/glossary-term/writing-supplement

[32] https://admission.princeton.edu/how-apply/application-checklist/princeton-supplement

[33] https://college.harvard.edu/sites/default/files/2020-07/harvard_fy_supplement_2020-2021_website.pdf

want to showcase your personality and passion while emphasizing the qualities that each college values.

The Writing Process

When I was in 3rd grade, I remember when my parents told me that writing was "my weakness." The parent-teacher meeting had gone well otherwise, but I couldn't stop focusing on the fact that I was a weak writer, according to my parents.

You may have also felt at some point in your life that you're bad at writing. In my opinion, that's like saying you're bad at art. First of all, that's a terrible thing to say to a young child, and second, those things are subjective and can be improved.

We all have a great writer inside us, but they're shy and can be nervous to come out and face the wall of criticism.

I once worked with a coaching student Heather, who was an amazing gymnast and wanted to apply to top schools as an English major. Her parents didn't believe in her writing potential, so when I coached her through the essay process, I realized that if she'd had as much coaching in writing as in her gymnastics, she might be a budding author by now.

There are two kinds of people: those who believe in talent and those who believe in putting in the hours. People who believe in talent are easily frustrated when they are naturally bad at things (which we all are - that's what a beginner is). Then there are people who believe in effort and how it can increase your skill. Let's use a Sally and Bob example.

Future Ivy

Sally has been told her whole life that she's gifted in computer science. She's faster than most of the other students. Bob has been told his whole life that he's a hard worker and can figure out anything when he sets his mind to it. He's picked up computer science at school and likes it.

Both students advance to take a college-level computer science class, which is challenging for both of them.

Who do you think will do better? Sally, who thinks she's naturally gifted, or Bob, who knows how to study hard? Who is more equipped to face challenges?

If you said Bob, you'd be right. While achievement is a mixture of talent and effort, at the end of the day, effort can trump talent. You could have the genes to be an award-winning runner, but if you don't practice, you won't set any school records. The same thing with writing. The more you practice, the better you'll get.

I know how hard it is to write the personal statement. I remember how lost and overwhelmed I felt about all the essays that schools wanted. I eventually got some help from teachers and an essay coach and was able to pull it all together. I learned the process the hard way and want to make it easier for you!

Here's your step by step plan to tackle the essay:

1. Brainstorm the topic
2. Pick the topic
3. Outline your essay
4. Write a first draft
5. Get feedback
6. Write your second draft

7. Get feedback
8. Write your third draft
9. Proofread and submit

After picking your topic, you'll want to write your sucky first draft. You might cringe after reading it, but know that writing is like sculpting. First, we get the general shape down, then we refine. I revised my essay 5+ times and have coached many students in college essays. With each revision, it gets closer to an essay that will wow your admissions officer and ensure that they remember you.

It's important to get feedback from people who are good writers and people you trust, like your English teacher, guidance counselor, or college essay coach. You may get conflicting feedback, so listen to your gut and put yourself in a tired admissions officer's shoes.

Just like when you do public speaking, it's important to know your audience when you write. According to former Ivy League admissions officer Harry Bauld, there are two kinds of admissions officers.[34] The senior folks, who he calls the "Lifers" and have been there for many years, and fresh admissions officers, which he calls "Temps" who likely just graduated from that school.

You don't know who will read your application, so instead make sure that your essay is accessible to all types of people. Maybe they can relate to your fascination with rolly pollies as a kid and they are impressed by your ability to take your curiosity into a career path. Writing your

---

[34] *On Writing the College Application Essay: The Key to Acceptance at the College of Your Choice* by Harry Bauld

personal statement will be hard, but you have many tries. A standout essay will be rewritten many times.

How to Brainstorm Your Essay Topic

You might be struggling to figure out what would be a good topic to share with the admissions officers. Is this a bad topic? You might ask yourself. One student reached out to me and asked me if writing a piece about his experience getting caught plagiarizing and doing a 180 from it would be a good idea. What do you think?

These are really great questions, and I'm going to help you figure out what is a good topic and what isn't. For example, say you're really interested in becoming a data scientist. You've always dreamed about this, because your uncle was a data scientist and he was a great mentor of yours.

You describe your motivation and your "why?" Why Data Science? You also show proof of your interest. In your essays, you talk about putting together conferences to spread awareness of data science careers to women and minorities. An essay describing your career motivations helps and will help win your admissions officers over.

Your admissions officer is trying to understand your personality and strengths, such as maybe you are incredibly resourceful or show great signs of leadership. These are just some of the many things that they look for, character qualities that they can see in your essays.

One way to pick the best topic is to first start with a long list of ideas. You can use some brainstorm questions or you can use the prompts in the supplemental and in the common application. After you go through the questions and note potential topics, you can run the best three ideas by your English teacher or your favorite teacher. It could also be your high school counselor. Having an objective perspective, especially from adults, can help you feel confident that it's a good topic.

A Cornell student I interviewed told me that the reason why she felt she was rejected from the other Ivy League colleges was because her essay repeated her resume and didn't really offer any glimpse into her life, what she would be like as a roommate, what she would be like as a student on campus, or what would she be like after graduating college and what she would contribute to her community.

I know you have a lot of great essays in you, so here are the three most important things to know when brainstorming your topic.

1) Brainstorming questions can help you find your unique perspective

Here are a few of my favorite ones to get the creative muscles going:

- What has been the hardest thing in your life?
- What in the world utterly fascinates you?
- Have you ever faced an ethical dilemma? How did you resolve it?
- What do you think of as your greatest victory?
- If you can't sleep at night, what's keeping you up?

2) Pick a topic that expands beyond your extracurricular list

Admissions officers want you to zoom in on a real slice of your life or a meaningful life experience that illuminates your unique personality and perspective.

Topics that have gotten people into the Ivy League include: passion for drumming, intellectual curiosity for writing, the generational immigrant experience, overcoming challenges such as a difficult home life, or experiences abroad.

3) Pick a topic that reveals your motivation, your "WHY"

What do people like Martin Luther King Jr., Steve Jobs, and the Wright Brothers have in common? They started with their "WHY" to inspire a movement. While you don't need to start a movement to get into your dream college, understanding your motivation and showing it in your essay can get the admissions officer on your side.

To find your motivation, ask yourself these questions: What gets you up in the morning? What keeps you up at night? Why do you do what you do?

For example, Apple's why is to challenge the status quo, to think differently by providing user-friendly innovative products.

My personal example of the "WHY" is to provide students with great career resources in order to get the best education and career-defining opportunities. Your "why" could be that you want ADHD to be a thing of the past and help people overcome it.

How to structure your essay

When I worked with students on their essays, I discovered a new way to structure essays so they are easy to outline and you overcome writer's block. This also makes the essays more interesting and more likely to make the admissions officers remember you.

Before you write your essay it's good to outline what you'd like to share with the reader in the essay. One way to do this is the IBPF method.

Structure your essay the IBPF way

- I for Intro - use an engaging hook.
- B for Body - where the storyline takes place.
- P for Point - what's your main lesson?
- F for Future - what's next for you? How does this connect with your goals and career plans?

For example, say that you are fascinated by psychology and you want to become a psychologist. After going through the brainstorm questions, you decide to write your essay about your experience interning with a psychologist and doing psychology research.

For the intro, you decide to start with a startling fact that relates to your research. For example, one of the essays in the book *50 Successful Harvard Application Essays* starts with "I shouldn't be here right now...There are 70 trillion genetic combinations to make human beings." Then, you decide to talk about the groundbreaking research that you've been involved with and struggled to get the information out to the practicing psychologists. You learned that to solve a problem, you need to start with awareness. And because of that, you decided that you wanted to be a psychologist and hope to connect the dots between groundbreaking research and clinical practice. You are ambitious, and you have shown that you are a leader and that you can find and create your own opportunities.

Move your action front and center

To keep your admissions officer engaged after reading thousands of yawn-inducing essays, make your essay stand out by cutting your descriptive intro and going right into the action.

For example, say your essay is about a being in a car accident. Instead of starting with "I was driving home from soccer practice and was on my way to the store for a slushie," start with the action: "White headlights flashed before me as I watched a car coming at me in the wrong lane." Another great intro that gets right into the action from one of the essays in the book *50 Successful Harvard Application Essays* is, "It was five o'clock in the morning, and an intruder was in my home." She then reveals the intruder was an automatic coffee maker replacing the fresh press.

In your conclusion, woo the college

Colleges value your genuine interest in the school, as the enrollment rate (number of people that enroll out of the accepted pool) matters for college rankings. This is why some colleges have a "Why this college" essay.

Even if this is not the "why this college" essay and you are using this for the personal statement, it's still great to personalize it to that university. To stand out, personalize your conclusion to reveal your career aspirations and what classes and activities you'd like to take advantage of at that specific school.

For example, "After taking CS50 online at Harvard, I felt strongly that I had found the perfect next step. I am excited to engage with the Innovation contest in the fall, connect with Professor Howard, and potentially intern at top tech companies."

Supplemental Essays

Why this school?

Future Ivy

When you fill out your application, some colleges may also ask you for a supplemental essay or short answers. One of the popular questions in the why us essay. The purpose of this essay is to gauge your level of interest in their school. For recruited athletes in particular, it's important to show your genuine interest, as the coaches only have a few spots.

When I was writing these essays, I made all the mistakes. I didn't personalize my "why us" essay, so you could switch out the names for another university and it didn't matter. I did no research on the universities. Honestly, I was so overwhelmed because I was applying to 21 schools and didn't get to tour any of them.

Now when I coach students through these essays, I see how much you can stand out with just a little basic research. For example, one of my coaching students was a psychology major and found the classes she wanted to take, the labs she wanted to do research in, and a mental health magazine that she wanted to be part of.

Who do you think stands out more? A writer who describes wanting to be challenged by the college-level classes and have access to "resources," or a student who tells you specific details of how they plan on being involved in the community?

So, how do you approach these essays? My favorite method and one that my students find simple is to split your essay into 3 parts: past, present, future.

You can first describe how you discovered your curiosity for your major, then write about what you've been doing to explore it further, whether that's clubs or internships, then describe what you plan to do at their university to further your studies in the major.

The specifics will help you stand out. Use their website, social media, and YouTube to learn more about the school and find specific programs, classes, and opportunities that excite you.

Short answers

It's sometimes harder to write these than the personal statement. Blaise Pascal said, "I have only made this letter longer because I have not had the time to make it shorter." When you only have 150 words or less, you will need to spend a lot of time cutting and rewriting to make your writing more concise.

Here are some tips to help you succeed:

- Don't repeat your activity list
- Do think about what character trait you want to portray, like your creativity
- Do use a small scene to make a point like a scene of you playing chess with your friend to show your passion for it
- Don't pick cliche broad topics like climate change or world peace
- Instead, be more specific to stand out, like combating the effects of nanoplastics in the environment.
- Like with the personal statement, getting feedback from people you trust and rewriting many times will help your short answers shine.

Summary

* In this chapter, you learned about the various types of essays you will be writing for your application and how they influence your admissions decision.
* You also learned how to brainstorm your essay topics and what topics to avoid.
* Finally, you learned some tips to structure your essay efficiently, how to get feedback, and how to answer the dreaded "why this school?" essay.

Action Steps

- [ ] Decide on the character qualities like resilience that you'd like to show in your essay
- [ ] Write your first draft
- [ ] Ask for feedback from your trusted friends and adults

CHAPTER 17

Ω

The Finishing Touches

Your letters of recommendation

I was scared. I had only been in my senior English teacher's class for two months, but I desperately needed a second letter of recommendation.

My Science/Math teacher was an easy first choice. I was in three of his classes, so he knew me well. But I couldn't ask my junior year English teacher because I felt like she didn't like me very much. I had to miss a lot of her class when I would go to debate tournaments and needed a lot of extensions on assignments.

I decided to ask my senior year English teacher after class, even though I had only been in her class for 2 months.

"Ms. K, I have a favor to ask. Could you please write me a letter of recommendation for college?" I asked.

A moment of silence. I could see by her expression that she was surprised. "I can, but I don't know you that well. Can you write to me what you'd like me to mention?" she responded.

"Yes, of course. Thank you so much! You'll have it by Friday." I said.

I was ecstatic but also confused. Did she want me to write the recommendation for her? Turns out, this is more common than I thought, and I highly encourage you to do something similar. I ended up writing an info sheet of my activities, goals, and how we first met in freshman year when I got an opportunity to network with her teacher friend, Mr. L, who used to be a lawyer.

She found this document super helpful and submitted a great letter of recommendation for me. This experience taught me a few things. The first is to identify the teachers who you want in junior year to write your letters of recommendation and make an effort to build relationships with them. Stay back after class to learn more about them and tell them some of the stuff you are working on.

The second thing is to provide your teachers with an info sheet. Even if they may know you very well, they have so many things going on - other students who are failing, school meetings they need to attend, and other letters of recommendation to write.

The easier you make it for them, the more likely it will be for them to submit it before the deadline. Most importantly, you'll get a super specific letter that mentions your application theme, your passion portfolio, and even some of your best qualities vs. a bland and generic statement from an overworked and underpaid teacher.

The info sheet

Your info sheet is the secret to getting a compelling recommendation letter that supports your story. Here are some bullets that would be great to include on your info sheet:

- Why you liked their class + a favorite project
- 3 of your best qualities
- Challenges you have overcome
- Your greatest accomplishments

- How you are different from your peers
- Your intended major
- Your list of schools
- Your extracurriculars

You might also attach your resume and college essay so they have more details to weave into their support letter.

Which teachers should I ask?

Always pick the teachers who you think genuinely like you. It's also good to pick one teacher related to your major, so if you are applying as a physics major, you can ask your physics teacher to recommend you. For the other teacher, most schools like to see a letter from an academic teacher, which means science, math, history, English, or language teachers.

Colleges typically like to see teachers from junior and senior year since those tend to be more advanced and closer in rigor to college classes. For example, since my theme was medical law, I had one recommendation letter from my physics/math (science) teacher and one from my English teacher (communication).

When do you ask?

You can ask your teachers at the end of junior year or beginning of senior year. Always give them at least 3+ weeks to do it and gently remind them closer to the deadline. A nice touch is to send your teachers a "thank you note," since they are doing you a favor and supporting you in your college journey.

Recommendations are extremely important, since the top schools have a lot of highly qualified academic students. Former assistant director of admissions at Dartmouth College, Michele Hernandez, reveals, "These letters are extremely important, because they let colleges see the student behind the grades and numbers."[35] These colleges want to understand what your participation in class is like, how you compare to all the other students the teacher has taught, and what you'd contribute to their college classrooms.

Now that you understand the importance of recommendation letters, maybe you are wondering how you can build a friendship with your teacher, especially if you are shy or socially awkward sometimes. Go back to Step 3 of ACHIEVE - help your teacher help you, and put the "avocado toast method" to work. Remember that this may take some time, but ultimately you just have to prepare and ask.

Here are some ideas to get started:

- Attend your teacher's office hours and bring one question from the homework or reading (you can bring a friend with you to make it less nerve-wracking the first few times).
- Prepare a question to ask in class by previewing the material before the lecture.
- Ask your teacher if you can become their assistant.
- The summer before the class, ask them for recommended readings and then discuss it in office hours.
- Participate in class by answering any questions you know or have a good guess on.
- Ask them what led them to become a teacher.

---

[35] *A Is for Admission: The Insider's Guide to Getting into the Ivy League and Other Top Colleges* by Michele A. Hernández

Interviews

I pulled up in front of my Harvard interviewer's house dressed in a blazer and black jeans. I had driven one hour to get here and was very nervous. This was Harvard's interview. I rang the doorbell and a tall Asian man dressed in a red sweater greeted me.

"Hi, um, I'm Amy. I'm here for my Harvard interview," I stuttered.

"Come in, we can sit in the kitchen," he motioned.

As I walked in, I saw military photos on his fridge and asked about them. He had gone to Harvard for undergrad and then became a doctor in the military.

After that, I remember being thrown questions like a hot potato.

"What's another hard question I could ask you?" he said after an hour.

After being put on the spot for the hardest grilling I've experienced, I thanked him and walked outside to my car. I felt I had done a good job fielding his questions, but it was exhausting.

This was one of many interviews I had during the admissions season. I remember two other interviews distinctly. One was my Dartmouth interview, where my interviewer asked me, "Why Dartmouth?" and I panicked and ended up answering with something generic. The other interview was for Tufts, and I sat in the wrong Starbucks for 20 minutes until I realized I was in the wrong spot. My interviewer was not impressed but agreed to wait for me to arrive at the correct location. I know interviewing is scary, but if you did look up the common app dataset for the relative importance of the interview, most times it's lower than the other things.

You might be wondering, what even are the interviews? When do they usually occur? What are their relevance to the application and acceptance process? I got you, Future Ivy!

Types of interviews

There are two types of interviews: on-campus and off-campus interviews. If your dream college offers on-campus interviews, which many top schools don't, make sure to reserve a spot as they are first come, first serve. Yale offers on-campus interviews by their college seniors who work at the admissions office.[36] If you aren't able to schedule an on-campus interview, you may have the chance to interview off-campus with an alumnus.

Off-campus interviews are generally coordinated by the alumni, previous students of the school, and offered to you depending on how many alumni volunteers are in your area. For example, as an alum of Harvard, I've personally interviewed students in my city's local high schools.

The importance of interviews

Your interview is only one part of your multi-faceted application, and if you aren't offered one, it's probably because there aren't enough volunteers in your area and you shouldn't worry. In Harvard's article "What to Expect at Your College Interview," they say, "your interview will never make or break your application; more likely than not, it'll just confirm that you're the awesome person that you showed you were in your application."

---

[36] https://admissions.yale.edu/interviews

For example, when I interviewed a graduating Harvard student who read their admission file, her interviewer described her as "super funny" and extremely "well-rounded," which helped her application stand out. Your interview is your chance to show your awesome personality and share your passion portfolio.

Interview timeline

This could vary depending on the school you are applying to and what their interview process looks like, so I'd suggest you research on their admissions' site.

In general, I've seen most schools follow the timeline on the MIT admissions site: Interviews are conducted from October through November for Early Action and December through January for Regular Action.[37] If you don't get an interview in that time period (and you are really interested in that school), you could reach out nicely to the admissions office and see if you can get an interview spot.

Tips for the interview

Here are some tips to impress your interviewer:

- Research your interviewer and ask hyper-targeted questions like, "I noticed on LinkedIn that you worked as a financial analyst after college, how did college prepare you?"
- Do research on the university and find specific reasons you want to go. For example, The Phillips Brook House, the center of community service at Harvard, might excite you.

---

[37] https://mitadmissions.org/help/faq/what-is-the-interview-process/

- Figure out why you and what you can contribute to the university. For example, you might be a mental health advocate at your school and want to continue this in college.
- Show up early and double-check the location. Some teachers in my life would say early is on time, on time is late. Make a good first impression by being early.
- Research common interview questions and prepare for them.

It's normal to be nervous in the interview. Your interviewer will understand that. This interview is a chance to add some color to your application, highlight your amazing personality, and help them help you by doing your prep. One of the Ivy League-admitted students I interviewed said she thought she bombed her interview, but when she read her admission file, her interviewer raved about her. Do your research, take some deep breaths, and do the best you can.

Summary

* In this chapter, you learned how letters of recommendation fit into your overall application, how to choose your recommenders, and that preparing an "info sheet" for your teachers is an amazing way to get a great letter of recommendation specific to your goals.
* You also learned how to prepare yourself for your interviews and some tips to make sure you make a great impression.

Action Steps

- ☐ Create an info sheet for your recommenders
- ☐ Research your interviewer and prepare questions
- ☐ Look up common interview questions and prepare responses beforehand

CHAPTER 18

Ω

The final stretch

There are very few decisions in life that change your trajectory, but applying to college is one of them. Whether you end up going to an Ivy to find your dream career in archaeology or to found your new company with a bunch of your roommates, or maybe you find your lifelong friends there, something big is waiting for you.

When I interviewed many Ivy League students and asked what their favorite thing was about college, they all mentioned the same thing - the diversity of people they met there. While you may get students from all around California in the UC system, in the Ivy League you end up meeting extraordinary people from around the globe. For example, my dormitory had the youngest published author in Zimbabwe, and we got to share stories from our past. I now have friends from all around the world.

You have a chance

The biggest question is, do you even have a chance? Is it like winning the lottery? While admission rates are intimidatingly low, you need to realize that just because it says 5% admissions doesn't mean you have a 5% chance.

Some applicants will have a 50% chance because they followed the standout mentality, and some applicants will have a 1% chance because they blend into the crowd. I know you can get into your dream school if you start applying the knowledge now and put in the hard work.

It's worth the hard work

You may want to get into the Ivies so that you can feel accomplished, make your parents proud, create a better life for your family, be a role model for others, have more job opportunities, or just earn the money to travel. Whatever your goal, the Ivy League can be a great way to get there.

For me, I wanted to make sure that I didn't struggle with money issues, since I grew up during a recession. Having an Ivy League degree got me into my first six-figure $100K+ job and has set me up to not worry about income. I have the financial security that I sought in high school! Whether you are seeking financial stability or wealth, the Ivy League name can help you stay competitive when the job market is tough. Not to mention the incredible classmates, professors, and all-around amazing people that you'll be interacting with at top schools. These are truly priceless connections that have made me who I am today.

The road ahead

Your days until you apply to college are numbered. While it may be three years or more, the time will fly by. You need to start as soon as possible to stand out among the crowd of applicants. Fortunately, you have some tools to supercharge your journey. You have the ACHIEVE system, so you know if you are on the right track and how to stay on the right track.

Toward the end of your junior year (the May before you apply), review the college application chapters to help you write your personal essay, ask for letters of recommendations, and prepare for your college interview.

It's also a good idea to chat with your parents about financial aid. Your tuition may vary depending on whether the college is in-state or out, private vs. public, and how generous their financial aid is. You can often get an estimate from the college website based on your family's income. One of my students from Michigan found that Yale was more affordable for them than an in-state public university.

When you apply will depend on whether you want to apply early or through regular admissions. There are two types of early admissions: early action and early decision. Early decision is binding, meaning that you must go if you are accepted. Dartmouth offers early decision and explains that you "are committing to attend Dartmouth if admitted."[38]

What your acceptance might look like

When Ivy day, the fated date of the admission results, came around, I was a wreck. My nerves were shot and the admissions emails were missing from my inbox. Heavy with disappointment, I made my way downstairs to eat a sadness sandwich.

As I took my first bite of remorse, my little sister came in and asked, "Did you hear from the Ivies?" I was so disappointed that I didn't respond, but she got the message. As she was walking away, I pulled my phone out with a full sandwich in my mouth. I refreshed my inbox to find nothing new. Then I peeked into my junk mail and saw an email from Harvard.

---

[38] https://admissions.dartmouth.edu/glossary-term/early-decision

I opened it and saw the word "Congratulations!" I called my sister back and yelled, "I got into Harvard!" She and I jumped up and down in excitement and squealed for over a minute, and my mom came down to join us in our celebratory moment.

I got into Harvard with a full scholarship and was excited for my future life, an easier one.

While some of admissions is luck, focusing on what you can control - studying for the ACT, SAT, getting high grades in your advanced courses, and pursuing career-exploring extracurriculars - does help. Harvard opened up a world of opportunities, from networking with the most ambitious and bright students to getting me a six-figure job ($100K+) after college.

My career in tech was fast-tracked and I want to help you unlock these opportunities too. You've learned what matters in your admission profile and how to market yourself in your application.

After you've hit the submit button and after many hours of revising your essays, researching your schools, and figuring out how to stand out, please take some time to celebrate. Applying to college is like running a marathon, regardless of your time after you finished!

"Not getting attached" mindset

One of my classmates always dreamed of going to Harvard. From 7th grade on she wore a Harvard sweatshirt and had a Harvard logo on her backpack. She would go on college tours to the Ivies and come back wearing more Harvard gear. When she didn't get in, she was devastated, even though she got into some other good schools.

I know it can be hard to not get attached to a school. It was easier for me, because I wasn't able to tour any schools before I applied.

Wherever you get in, it will be okay. Maybe you wanted to get into Columbia and instead you got into Brown. College is what you make of it.

Also, colleges range drastically in their financial aid policies, so sometimes you get into your dream school but can't afford it.

I promise it will all work out in the end. The world rewards those that are driven and hardworking like you. There will be more opportunities to shoot for, like grad school.

You will succeed in whatever you do when you set your mind to it, but don't focus on what you can't control.

You can't control whether a college accepts you, but you can do your best to keep up your impact in your community so that if they waitlist you, you will have significant updates to your accomplishments. You can continue to network and find internships that catalyze your career.

You can't control the outcome, but you can control your reaction to it. You've got this!

You did it!

Through this book, we built a house of knowledge so that you can have an easier time navigating the labyrinth of top college admissions. You learned the foundation of standing out and how to make a great first impression. You put up the walls and the roof with the ACHIEVE system and built a passion portfolio. You painted, decorated, and prepared the house for sale by learning how to write the college essays, how to approach the college interview, and how to get the best letters of recommendations. Lastly, we sold the house and moved onto the next one when you learned how to submit your application and get accepted.

Summary

* In this last practical chapter, you learned that deciding to go to an Ivy League college is one of the most important decisions you'll make in your life. It will be very tough, and you will be pushed way out of your comfort zone, but it's so worth it, and you do have a chance.
* Above all, you can rest assured that if you follow the steps in this book, you can guarantee that you will have clarity about what you want to do with your life. At the end of the process, you will become the kind of person that succeeds for the rest of your life, no matter what college you get into.

Action Steps

- ☐ Research the costs of your each college you want to apply to
- ☐ Decide if you want to apply early or regular decision
- ☐ Prepare your mindset so you don't get attached to one school

CHAPTER 19

π

NEXT STEPS

You have just learned that it is possible to beat the odds and stand out in your application to get into an Ivy League college. It takes a lot of hard work, relationship building, asking questions, and ultimately time. Notice that I didn't mention "tears," because I believe that you can do this with much less stress. The admissions and applications process is normally so complicated that I wouldn't recommend you try to figure it out on your own. With this book, I'm hoping to save you tons of time by providing all the skills and tools I used and wish I knew in high school to get accepted into multiple Ivy League colleges and eventually graduate from Harvard University.

Great, so now what?

To take the first step, you must take a step back and look at your high school accomplishments through your new Future Ivy lenses. You must be honest and recognize where you are on the ACHIEVE system, decide where you want to be, and follow the checklist in this book to get into your dream school.

If you are a junior-senior at a rigorous school, you might find that you've already taken the most advanced classes, done a time audit, feel comfortable with the SAT, and developed friendships with your favorite teachers. This means that you are doing pretty well on the -A-C-H- but still have some work to do on the -I-E-V-E- steps, with defining your project, theme, reaching out to professionals, and creating an impact. I still recommend you start at the beginning and keep in mind that this is a checklist and you can go back and forth as much as you need to, as long as at the end of the day, you're checking off all the boxes.

It's tough to say when it's too late or if you've missed your chance because of low grades earlier on, but I still believe that if you have a strong enough "why", an amazing project that is preparing you for a future career, and the dedication to put your phone on airplane mode for hours of studying and helping others, then it's never too late. I pulled my application together junior year and studied for the ACT for 3 months. It was absolutely grueling and I wouldn't recommend it, but I'm saying it's possible. I had a very clear goal, a burning "why", an innate desire to take advanced classes, teach debate, and ask tons of questions.

If you're a freshman/sophomore planning your classes, you would naturally start by focusing on step A and getting into advanced classes, then C, cutting activities that distract you from your main goals. Next, you would gradually build your relationships with your teachers by asking questions and talking to them about your interests with step H (helping your teachers help you). Continue following your curiosity to I - Ignite your interests and interview professionals to understand the job. As you learn about your passion, you can share your journey by executing your themed project with step E (execute your theme), hopefully in a way that helps your community and relies on your strengths. By the time you get to V (validate your credibility), you may already be a junior/senior and you'll have enough experience in your subject to be featured as a rising influencer. Finally, once you're a Junior, you'll know the ins and outs of the SAT/ACT and earn your target score, or step E, completing the ACHIEVE system and setting yourself up for a life of success.

Future Ivy

For most students I coach, the biggest gap is in steps C-H-I-E-V, where their biggest obstacle, besides having way too many activities (hence C), is the execution of their project and talking with real professionals to understand their career options. You'll discover when you look through your Future Ivy lenses that any gap can be closed by having focus.

Since I started sharing my lessons learned from going through the Ivy League 7+ years ago, I have helped hundreds of students and friends understand and bridge their gaps in terms of standing out.

And remember…

You can achieve anything you set your mind to!

-Amy Jin, Your Ivy league guide

San Francisco, CA

Closing Remarks

As my mentor Jon Rahoi would say, there are two kinds of mindsets: fishing and hunting.

Hunters have a single focus on a type of prey. They spend hours, days, months preparing for a single shot and will go home hungry if they miss their target.

People who fish cast out a net and are open to different kinds of catches be it a rock fish or a striped bass. They stay open to the many opportunities of the sea.

This is important in your college journey as there are many schools beyond the Ivy League that can bring you closer to your goals.

Cast a wide net beyond the Ivies so you have plenty of other options to choose from. Stay open to opportunities that you may not have expected. For example, some schools offer their top applicants more scholarships or first pick of their classes. Also, prestige doesn't equal fit. Maybe you find during college visits that you prefer the small liberal arts vibe of Amherst or Middlebury College.

While I focus on getting into the Ivies, you can use this book to stand out to your dream schools whether they are competitive schools like Stanford, MIT, or University of Chicago or your local state school that offers you great merit scholarships.

So my question to you is, are you going to hunt or fish?

Future Ivy

Appendix A

ACHIEVE system checklist

A- Aim for As in advanced classes

- Get into the most advanced classes at your school
- Get As in most classes
- Create a 4 year plan of classes with your counselor
- See if dual enrollment is an option by talking to your guidance counselor

C- Conduct an Activity Audit

- Conduct a "Class time audit"
- Conduct an "extracurricular time audit"
- Cut down to 1-2 main activities
- Every time you feel overwhelmed, do another activity audit

H- Help your teacher help you

- Send a thank you email to teachers you talk to
- Participate 1x in every class (it could be asking a question)
- Note down ways you can help make your teacher's life easier.
- Go to 3 teacher's office hours/ schedule 1-1 (Talk about your career choice)

I- Ignite your interests

- Take an aptitude test online
- Reflect on careers that combine your interests

- Reach out to 10 professionals in the fields that you are interested online/or through family/friends/counselor
- Interview 2 professionals via zoom

E- Execute your theme

- Define your application theme
- Identify which types of projects you want in your passion portfolio
- Narrow down to one project to start
- Brainstorm people who may be able to advise your project and ask them

V- Validate your credibility

- Brainstorm 3 ways that you increase your impact and bolster your credibility
- Pitch 5 local publication or magazines related to your project
- Keep track of your accomplishments every semester by writing your resume bullets using result + action

E- Earn your SAT scores

- Decide which test to take SAT vs ACT
- Schedule your test dates, plan to take 2x official test
- Schedule 1x full practice exam per week 8x
- Analyze your wrong answers and write out what you would do next time

Future Ivy

Exclusive free video course for Future Ivy readers!!!

♥

Learn the 5 most important things in your admission journey

- How to know what admission factor is more important
- How to find scholarships
- What type of extracurriculars do admissions officers value?
- Advice for writing college essays
- Common app walkthrough

Future Ivy

Want Amy to keynote for your next event?

Inquire for more details at Ivyleagueguidellc@gmail.com

As a high school student, Amy made the impossible seem possible. Amy prepared herself for top colleges in the obvious ways, while simultaneously pursuing opportunities that undoubtedly made her applications POP! The good news for you: she's condensed it into a practical, seven step guide for success.

— Brett Sklove, High School Counselor

Future Ivy

Acknowledgements

α

Thank you to all my friends, family, and those who have supported me in this book; I couldn't have done it without you.

To all the people I interviewed, thank you for sharing your journey with me so that more students can stand out to their dream schools!

My team – Luis, Jay, and Meb. I'm so grateful to have your creative talents and your positive spirits.

My friends and goal-getters - Madeline, Rachel, Erin, and Megan. You inspire me to dream bigger and hustle harder.

My loves Luis, Boo, and Papaya - you make every day shine brighter with your encouragement and playfulness!

Future Ivy

About the Author

∞

Amy Jin is a Harvard grad and college admissions coach who specializes in helping students stand out to the Ivy League and other top colleges. Her students have gotten into many top schools like Harvard, MIT, Caltech, UCLA, and Berkeley.

In high school, she learned the art of debating and loved it so much that she ended up teaching it. Amy was voted "most likely to come back as a teacher" by her high school class.

Having learned the Ivy league application process and gotten in, she wanted to pass this forward as well.

She shares more career and college-readiness content on her Youtube, Tiktok and Instagram to 50K+ people. Her mission is to be the college and career center in every student's pocket!

Ivyleagueguidellc@gmail.com
IG @ivyleagueguide
Tiktok @ivyleagueguide
Youtube @ivyleagueguide

Printed in Great Britain
by Amazon